K

Logic With Added Reasoning

D1738796

Logic With Added Reasoning

Michael J. Gabbay

King's College, University of London

broadview press

National Library of Canada Cataloguing in Publication Data

Gabbay, Michael
        Logic with added reasoning / Michael Gabbay

(The Broadview library of logic and critical thinking)
Includes index.

ISBN 1-55111-405-4

1. Logic. 2. Truth. I. Title. II. Series: Broadview library of logic and critical thinking.

BC177.G32 2002   160   C2002-902036-0

Broadview Press Ltd., is an independent, international publishing house, incorporated in 1985. Broadview believes in shared ownership, both with its employees and with the general public; since the year 2000 Broaadview shares have traded publicly on the Toronto Venture Exchange under the symbol BDP.

We welcome comments and suggestions regarding any aspect of our publications—please feel free to contact us at the addresses below or at broadview@broadviewpress.com.

North America
P.O. Box 1243, Peterborough, Ontario, Canada K9J 7H5
3576 California Road, Orchard Park, NY 14127
Tel: (705) 743-8990; Fax: (705) 743-8353
e-mail: customerservice@broadviewpress.com

UK, Ireland, and contintental Europe
Thomas Lyster, Ltd., Units 3 & 4a, Old Boundary Way
Burscough Road, Ormskirk
Lancashire L39 2YW
Tel: (01695) 575112; Fax: (01695) 570120
e -mail: books@tlyster.co.uk

Australia and New Zealand
UNIREPS, University of New South Wales
Sydney, NSW, 2052
Tel: 61 2 9664 0999; Fax: 61 2 9664 5420
e-mail: info.press@unsw.edu.au

www.broadviewpress.com

Broadview Press gratefully acknowledges the financial support of the Government of Canada through the Book Publishing Industry Development Program for our publishing activities.

PRINTED IN CANADA

For you

Contents

Pre-Preface

- The less common truth functional notation is chosen as it is almost never used to denote anything other than the classical operators. Similarly for the quantifier notation.

- This book contains only one small footnote pertaining to set theory (page 30).

- Mention or formal theory of the following terms occur only here:

  Axiom
  Completeness
  Consistency
  Domain
  Model
  Non-Classical
  Proof (except in the term "indirect proof" which is explained)
  Semantics
  Soundness (except with reference to arguments)
  Syntax

  Most of the above terms are considered informally.

- Decidability is mentioned (by name only in the index) briefly at the end. "Deduction system" is used non-technically. Indirect proof and reductio are explained and differentiated informally.

- Understanding of the quantifiers is substitutional (but not by definition) (see Ignorance below).

- Quantification is explicitly over non-empty domains (not in those words).

Ignorance

Some tangential points stated in the text are avoided. Look under Ignorance in the index and find reference to ignoring in the text.

Preface

This book is based on the excellent lecture series by Dr. Tony Dale. I have to thank him for his extreme generosity with his time, effort and experience in his detailed criticisms and suggestions.

The whole point of the logic we shall develop is to provide a tool for doing mathematics and philosophy (in other words, thought). The way in which logic acts as a tool is that it does a lot of thinking for you. For example, someone else has done a lot of work to produce an automatic screwdriver so that most of the work involved is done for you.[1] It is just like this with a logic; it is generated so that half the work involved in thinking is done for you by something else, the rules and laws of the logic.

Logic tries to provide a mechanical and methodical way of performing some otherwise complicated thought operations whilst preserving the results these complicated operations yield.[2] Bearing this in mind here are a few tips on how to study logic and its use:

- Logic is designed to be mechanical, so when you are spewing out a logical argument, think like a machine. The trick with logic is to follow all the rules and do no more than what they tell you to do.

- When writing down any piece of logic do not be afraid to be over-specific and pedantic about what you say. In logic you can NEVER over-specify. You must always assume that the person who is going to read your logic is completely ignorant.

- Make absolutely certain that you understand everything there is to understand about valid arguments (Chapter 1) before going any further with the book.

- If you spend more than 10 minutes trying to understand any paragraph in this book, stop thinking, put the book down, and do something mindless

---

[1] To the disappointment of many, much screwing is now automatic.

[2] Because of this, many people rather stupidly believe that doing too much logic will turn one into Mr Spock, devoid of all original thought and ideas. Not only is it untrue that logic will turn you into anything like Mr Spock, it is certainly false that Mr Spock should have to be devoid of all original thought and ideas. Logic helps you think methodically and with structure; in any situation such an ability is invaluable.

for at least half an hour. Then ignore it since everything is repeated in a number of different ways.

- Do not strain yourself working. With any subject that involves understanding it is silly to work too hard. Possibly not so much with logic but certainly with philosophical understanding (of which you will need a little to do logic), too much work will lead you to get it wrong. Anyway, within the book all the content is rewritten in numerous forms.

- If you find the logic in the book easy to grasp, then go ahead and take a course in Set Theory and more advanced Symbolic Logic.

- Make other people do logic.

- Falsity should be taken very seriously.[3] If there is anything you notice in the book that you think is incorrect, send an e-mail.

- Any comments, compliments and stuff, send an e-mail.

- Logic will NOT make you boring.

- Try not to be as patronizing as this preface.

---

[3] See Exodus, Chapter 23, Verse 7.

Chapter 1

Arguments and Validity

1.1 Validity and Arguments

1.1.1 A little argument

Whenever we talk to anyone else we will inevitably find ourselves using an argument of some kind. The argument is essentially there to convince our interlocutor of whatever opinion we may hold. Merely asserting an opinion without giving it any kind of backing is rarely enough to convince anyone of its truth. A well-reasoned argument is certainly the the best, and least violent method by which one can convince others of one's opinions. Clearly the difference between convincing someone and not convincing them with an argument is how good the argument is; the better the argument the more likely it is to convince. It is a basic purpose of logic to be able to provide a method by which all arguments can be evaluated. This claim may be (and is) disputed; it is a matter of great debate between logicians and philosophers as to what the purpose and meaning behind a logic system actually is. What is undeniable however is that the ability to evaluate arguments (practical human argument as well as formal mathematical reasoning) is vital for the logic system to be of any use.

We need to clarify what constitutes a "good" argument. Intuitively speaking, when we say that a particular argument is good we may mean a number of distinct things:

1. That every statement in the argument is coherent and meaningful.

2. That the assumptions the argument uses are plausible or acceptable.

3. The conclusion of the argument follows from its assumptions.

(1) and (2) are both important for the argument to be convincing. Certainly (1) is very important and is necessary for any conversation whatsoever. However (2) is not as important as it looks. It is not that important for an argument that its assumptions are plausible to everyone who sees them. It may be the case

that the assumptions seem completely ridiculous and unacceptable and yet be true. Indeed, it is not even necessary that the assumptions are true. Consider the lawyer who argues on the side of a guilty man; even though something has to be wrong with some of his assumptions (as the man is guilty), one can still say his arguments were good. What is important is (3), that the conclusion should follow from the premises.

This notion of following from the premises is called the *validity* of the argument. An argument is valid if its conclusion follows from its premises. It is important to note that to say an argument is valid and to say it is good are two different things. The *validity* of an argument does not take into account whether the premises are true or plausible. The first concern of any logic dealing with arguments is to get a formal definition of *validity*. In order to do this it is necessary to consider the structure that arguments can take. Consider the argument within the following dialogue.

A: Abortion should be illegal.
B: Why?
A: Because it is the killing of a foetus.
B: So what?
A: The foetus is human and the killing of humans should be illegal.

The argument involves two premises (one has two parts) and a conclusion. This is in fact how an argument is defined:

Definition 1.1.1 *An argument is a set of premises and a conclusion. All the sentences in an argument must be statements that can be true or false.*[1]

The premises are that abortion is the killing of a foetus, the foetus is human, and that killing of humans should be illegal. The conclusion is that abortion should be illegal. Many people would say that this argument is not a good one and that the conclusion is wrong: abortion should not be illegal. What opponents say is wrong with the argument is that at least one of the premises is false. It is said that the foetus is not human, but it could also be said that the foetus is not killed (it never was alive), or that there should not be a blanket law against killing humans. But we cannot deny the conclusion of the argument by saying that the conclusion does not follow from the premises, because it does. It is important to note that the fact that the conclusion follows from the premises is totally independent of whether they are true. Whether or not a foetus is human, killing humans should be illegal, or the foetus is actually killed, the conclusion still follows from the premises. The validity of an argument is a

---

[1] For example:

Peter love
Predominant
Fat

is not an argument.

relation between the premises and the conclusion and does not take into account whether any of them are true.

1.1.2   A theory of validity

It is now necessary to give some account of what it means for the conclusion to follow from the premises. It seems that we mean that, given the premises, we cannot deny the conclusion; you have to accept the conclusion if you accept the premises. This makes a very good definition of validity indeed.

Definition 1.1.2 *An argument is valid when there is no way for the premises to be true and the conclusion to be false (remember that validity means the conclusion follows from the premises).*

This definition is not as straightforward as it sounds. It is not absolutely clear what the "there is no way" means. What is a way? For our purposes there is no way for *A* to be true when no matter what the universe is like *A* is false. When we look at various ways *A* might be true, we can have the laws of physics as crazy as we like, and the Universe can contain as many or as few objects as we like. *There is no way for the premises to be true while the conclusion is false when in all the crazy and the not so wild universes the conclusion is true if the premises are true.*

This idea of there being no way is related but is not to be confused with *necessity*. Necessity is often required to be a little more sensitive. For example we may hold that the laws of physics are necessary, but there is a crazy universe in which the laws of physics do not hold (there is a way for the laws of physics not to be true). Sometimes philosophers will use the word "necessary" to mean "no way" as we have defined it; on many other occasions, philosophers will mean something else. Very often validity and following out of necessity are not equivalent (but if "necessity" is being used to mean "no way" as above, then validity and following out of necessity are equivalent).[2]

Let us make an example of a well known argument:

> All men are mortals
> Socrates is a man
> therefore Socrates is mortal.

If all men are mortals and Socrates is a man then clearly there is no way Socrates is not going to be a mortal. If you say, "Maybe Socrates is a special kind of immortal man," then you are contradicting the first premise, that ALL men are mortals. So there is no way in which the premises are true and the conclusion false; thus the argument is valid.

---

[2]Upon seeing the word "necessary" or "impossible" great care should be taken. In a text like this, usually any such use is equivalent to "in all ways," "in no way," and "there is a way" respectively.

1.2   Examples of valid and invalid arguments

When we speak of an argument being good or even sound, we mean that it is valid and has true premises. Validity ignores whether the premises are true or false; it does not matter if the conclusion states that pigs can fly. Validity is only concerned with whether the conclusion, whatever it is, follows from the premises, whatever they are. An argument is valid when the conclusion MUST be true IF the premises are true. Here are some more examples of valid and invalid arguments:

1.2.1   Valid arguments

Premise:	All cats are mammals	True	
Premise:	All mammals are vertebrates	True	Valid
Conclusion:	All cats are vertebrates	True	

	All cats are carnivores	True	
	All carnivores are mammals	False	Valid
	All cats are mammals	True	

	All cats are carnivores	True	
	All carnivores are dogs	False	Valid
	All cats are dogs	False	

	All cats can fly	False	
	All flying things are vegetarians	False	Valid
	All cats are vegetarians	False	

	All cats can fly	False	
	All flying things are mammals	False	Valid
	All cats are mammals	True	

Arguments of this type are called *syllogisms*.[3] They are the basic form of argument and analysis of them has dated as far back as Aristotle. In fact, Aristotle thought all arguments could be somehow reduced to a syllogism,[4] a claim that is now very much out of date.

All the above arguments are valid because there is no way their premises could be true without the conclusion also being true.

It should be noted that an argument *may be valid even if the premises are all false and the conclusion is true*. The validity of the argument does not depend on the truth or falsity of its premises and conclusion.

---

[3]There are strict conditions for an argument to be a syllogism which will be dealt with partially in Chapter 9.

[4]See the *Prior Analytics*.

1.2.2 Invalid arguments

Take a look at these arguments:

Some lecturers are logicians	True	
Some logicians like cats	True	Invalid
Some lecturers like cats	True	

All humans are mammals	True	
Some mammals are dogs	True	Invalid
Some humans are dogs	False	

The last two examples are invalid because their conclusions do not follow necessarily from the premises. There is a simple way of determining the invalidity of an argument if you do not recognize it outright (the last example is clearly invalid as it actually does have true premises and a false conclusion; if it were valid, this would be impossible). If you can imagine a situation in which the premises are true and the conclusion is false, then the argument is invalid. If you cannot find such a situation, then the argument is probably valid (but this is not guaranteed as you may not be looking at the right situations). Let us see how this may work:

All cats are purple
All fish are purple
Some cats are fish

Is this argument valid or invalid? Both the premises and the conclusion are clearly false. *This however has no bearing at all on whether or not the argument is valid,* as validity has nothing whatsoever to do with the truth values of the sentences in the argument. Let us try to create a situation in which the premises are true and the conclusion is false; if we can, the argument is invalid.

It is not that difficult to imagine a world in which all cats are purple and so are all fish. Does it have to be that there are some cats in this world that are fish? No, it does not have to be like that. Suppose all the cats are gathered together in a group, and all the fish are gathered together in a separate group. It is quite reasonable for all of them to be purple without any being a member of both groups. So we now have a situation in which all cats are purple, all fish are purple, and no cat is a fish; the argument is invalid. But we need not talk in terms of cats and fish. Let us restate the argument using slightly different animals:

All bachelors are unmarried
All spinsters are unmarried
Some bachelors are spinsters

Now the argument's invalidity becomes clear: it *is* true that all bachelors are unmarried and true that all spinsters are unmarried. But if the argument were valid, then it would follow that some bachelors are spinsters and that is clearly false. It is quite possible for every x to be y and every z to be y without any x being z.

1.3   Validity and the structure of an argument

1.3.1   Validity is independent of meaning

We have just observed a very important fact. Not only is validity independent
of what truth values the statements take, it is also independent of what objects
and properties the statements are about. Whether we talk about cats being
humans, bachelors being unmarried or every x being y the argument is still
valid. So if we have any syllogism that is valid we can interchange the terms as
much as we like and maintain the validity. The reason for this is quite simple.
Validity is a relation between the premises and the conclusion, it is concerned
only with the structure of the argument. Which particular terms ("mammals" is
a term) the argument uses has nothing to do with the structure of the argument,
so validity is not affected by meaning.[5] However, if we have a syllogism which
is invalid, then it is *not* the case that no matter how we change the terms it will
remain invalid. Take the following example:

> All dogs are carnivores
> All cats are cute
> ───────────────
> All dogs are cute

The above argument is clearly invalid. However, see what happens when we
change the term "cute" for "dogs." We get the following argument:

> All dogs are carnivores
> All cats are dogs
> ───────────────
> All dogs are dogs

This new argument is valid because the conclusion, "All dogs are dogs" is necessarily true. There is no way the premises can be true and the conclusion false
(because the conclusion cannot be false).

Have a look at the following arguments:

> All cats are mammals
> All mammals are vertebrates
> ───────────────
> All cats are mammals

This argument is valid, just as this argument:

> All Martians are jazz pianists
> All jazz pianists have shabby hair   (All jazz pianists are shabby-haired things[6]
> ───────────────
> All Martians have shabby hair   (All Martians are shabby-haired things)

Also valid is:

> All Splogs are Queebles
> All Queebles like Gloobies   (All Queebles are Gloobie-likers)
> ───────────────
> All Splogs like Gloobies   (All Splogs are Gloobie-likers)

---

[5] Admittedly, there is the case of the following type of argument:

> Roderick is a bachelor
> ───────────────
> Roderick is unmarried

which is valid and does depend on the meanings of the terms. Please ignore such cases.

[6] "All jazz pianists have shabby hair" is true when "all jazz pianists are things with shabby
hair" is true. In these cases we may interchange the sentences without affecting the argument.

Similarly, this argument is valid:

> All x are y
> All y are z
> ‾‾‾‾‾‾‾‾‾‾‾
> All x are z

This gives us a very easy way of determining the validity and invalidity of arguments.

1.3.2 Determining validity by changing to an easier meaning

Since it does not matter whether the argument uses Martians that are Queebles or As that are Bs, we can take a set of neutral terms and compare any argument with an argument of the same form using those neutral terms. We have already come across a set of neutral terms, the letters of the alphabet. So we can take any argument and change its terms into letters of the alphabet and see if it has a structure that is valid.

> All cats are mammals
> Some mammals have tails   (Some mammals are things that have tails etc.)
> ‾‾‾‾‾‾‾‾‾‾‾‾‾‾‾‾‾‾‾
> Some cats have tails

We can turn this into an argument using letters without affecting its validity:

> All A are B
> Some B are C
> ‾‾‾‾‾‾‾‾‾‾
> Some A are C

In this more neutral form the argument is easier to analyze. We can now substitute easier meanings for the letters. Here is my favourite easy meaning:

> All bachelors are unmarried people
> Some unmarried people are spinsters
> ‾‾‾‾‾‾‾‾‾‾‾‾‾‾‾‾‾‾‾‾
> Some spinsters are bachelors

As long as the structure is not altered, we can change the terms of the syllogism (or any other argument) as much as we like, and the validity, if the argument is valid, will be unaffected.

> All logicians are mad   All A are B
> Some philosophers are logicians =   Some C are A
> ‾‾‾‾‾‾‾‾‾‾‾‾‾‾‾‾‾‾‾   ‾‾‾‾‾‾‾‾‾
> Some philosophers are mad   Some C are B

This argument is valid. If there is a C which is an A, and every A is a B, then the C (which is also an A) must also be a B. What can be done now is to learn all possible forms of syllogisms and compare any argument to a memorized argument involving letters of the alphabet. This strategy is not recommended as not all arguments are syllogisms, and it would certainly be better to understand what exactly is going on.

1.4   Other forms of argument

1.4.1   Modus Ponens and friends

Almost all of the arguments we have looked at so far have been syllogisms. There are many other different types of argument. Validity applies to them all in exactly the same way. Here is another form of valid argument that is similar to those we have just seen.

> Socrates is a man
> If Socrates is a man, then Socrates is mortal
> _____
> Socrates is mortal

This form of argument should be quite familiar; we use it all the time in our natural deductive reasoning and it is quite obviously valid. Any argument of this form is valid.

> A
> If A then B .
> _____
> B

This form of argument is called Modus Ponens and is used not only as the classic example of a valid argument but as the basis of almost all logic systems. There is a famous fallacy (a fallacy is an argument that looks valid but really is not) related to Modus Ponens.

> B
> If A then B
> _____
> A

This is a famous invalid argument (sometimes jokingly called Modus Morons) and is called *The fallacy of affirming the consequent*.[7]

1.4.2   More valid arguments

Is the following argument valid?

> This logic book is great
> This logic book is not great
> _____
> The sky is blue

It is very easy to make the mistake of jumping in too soon and stating that the argument is not valid because the conclusion has nothing to do with the premises. If we look at Def 1.1.2 we see that nothing is mentioned about the conclusion having anything to do with the premises. All that validity requires is that there is no way for the premises all to be true and the conclusion to be false. With this in mind, is there a way for the premises both to be true? The answer is that it is impossible for this book to be both great and not great. If it

_____

[7]In a conditional like "If A then B," A is called the *antecedent* and B is called the *consequent*.

is impossible for the premises to be true, then it is impossible for the premises to be true while the conclusion is false.[8] The argument is *valid*.

It is true that if we replace the conclusion with any statement we like we would still have a valid argument. This illustrates a famous point of logic: from a contradiction (the two premises contradict each other, which is why they cannot both be true), we can form a perfectly valid argument and deduce anything and everything. There is a famous example illustrating this. Bertrand Russell was once asked if he could deduce from the statement $2 + 2 = 5$ that he was the pope. Russell replied with the following argument:[9]

1. Suppose $2 + 2 = 5$

2. Subtracting 2 from both sides of the equation we get $2 = 3$

3. Transposing, we get $3 = 2$

4. Subtracting 1 from both sides, we get $2 = 1$

5. Now, the pope and I are two. Since two equals one, then the pope and I are one. Hence I am the pope.

Here is another argument (we have seen its kind before):

> Raw cabbage is a good aid for sunbathing
> Being tall in public is illegal
> All cats are cats

Is this argument valid? Is it possible for the premises to be true and the conclusion false? Of course not. Since it is impossible for the conclusion to be false, it is necessarily true (here "necessarily true" means is true in all ways, in all the crazy and sane universes) that all cats are cats (it can not be that there is a cat that is not a cat). This means that it is impossible for the premises to be true and the conclusion false, it is simply impossible for the conclusion to be false.

1.4.3 Conclusions

To recapitulate: an argument is valid when the conclusion must be true if you accept that the premises are true. The validity of an argument has no bearing whatsoever on the meanings or the actual truth values of the sentences involved. It is just the structure of the argument that counts; as a result, it is possible to change the meaning (not the structure) of the argument completely without affecting its validity. It is this notion of validity that is the most important of all the notions involved in argumentation. As we shall see, it is the main purpose of logic to produce a system by which we can analyze argument and the structure of language independently of meanings.

---

[8] It is also impossible for the premises to be true while the conclusion is true. However we do not care about this. If it cannot be that the premises are true and the conclusion is false then the argument is valid.

[9] To my knoweldge and that of Russell experts I consulted, this is not a direct quotation from Russell. I paraphrase from (probably another paraphrase in) Raymond Smullyan's *What is the name of this book?* (Penguin, 1990).

1.5   Exercises

An argument is *valid* when it is impossible for its premise(s) to be true and its conclusion false. An argument is invalid otherwise.

Judge whether the following arguments are valid or invalid. If you judge an argument to be invalid briefly state why.

1. Some cats eat fish
    Some fish-eaters have tails

    Some cats have tails

2. All opponents must be beaten
    Some opponents are objectors

    Some objectors must be beaten

3. John ran quickly

    John ran

4. Somebody loves everybody

    Everybody is loved by somebody

5. Everybody loves somebody

    Somebody is loved by everybody

6. Today is Tuesday
    The husband is happy only if it is Tuesday

    The husband is happy

7. The wife is happy
    The wife is happy only if the game has been cancelled

    The game has been cancelled

8. Elvis liked Fool's Gold

    A man called 'Elvis' liked Fool's Gold

Chapter 2

Truth Functionality

2.1 Embedded sentences

2.1.1 Basic and simple sentences found in larger sentences

Some sentences have other sentences embedded in them. That is, it is possible to find within some English sentences another (shorter) meaningful sentence.

Definition 2.1.1 *For any two sentences A and B, say that sentence B is embedded in sentence A when all the words that make up B can be found in A in the right order and all together. Note that according to this definition every sentence is embedded in itself, but we shall ignore this.*

Definition 2.1.2 *Now, B is a* main embedded sentence *of A when B is embedded in A and B is embedded in no other sentence embedded in A (aside from A itself). A main embedded sentence of A is a sentence that is within A and is as least embedded.*

- Consider the sentence "Snow is white." This sentence has no other meaningful sentences embedded in it.

- However the sentence "Peter believes that snow is white" does contain the embedded sentence "Snow is white."

- "Grass is green and Peter believes that snow is white" is a sentence with three embedded sentences (aside from itself). Further it has two main embedded sentences: "Grass is green" and "Peter believes that snow is white."

It does not matter that when you remove the embedded sentence what remains is not meaningful ("Peter believes that" is not really a sentence) as we are not splitting up the sentence, we are just spotting the parts of larger sentences that are meaningful sentences in themselves.[1]

- The sentence "It is not the case that snow is white" also contains the (main) embedded sentence "Snow is white."

- The sentence "Both snow is white and is grass is green" contains two (main) embedded sentences.

- The sentence "Jane said that grass is green and snow is white" contains three embedded sentences: "grass is green," "snow is white" and "grass is green and snow is white." Only one of these three is a main embedded sentence.[2]

The sentence "Snow is not white" does not contain the embedded sentence "Snow is white"; the embedded sentence must be complete and not split up. However the sentence "Snow is not white" has exactly the same meaning as "It is not the case that snow is white" which does have an embedded sentence.

The first logic system we shall develop is called *truth functional logic* or *propositional logic*. It deals with embedded sentences and provides a logic for how they can interact with each other.

2.1.2   Truth values

In this system of logic any statement, embedded or not, can take truth values. In propositional logic there are only two possible truth values: true and false. The sentence "Snow is white" is true if snow is in fact white and the sentence is false if snow is not.

2.1.3   Propositions

It may be confusing that we speak of propositional logic but talk little about propositions. In fact we shall be doing our logic on sentences rather then propositions. Even then we shall only be dealing with sentences that make statements (as opposed to a sentence that asks a question). It would perhaps be less confusing to call it *sentential logic* instead of propositional logic but the latter name is more common.

A proposition is usually taken to be that which is common to sentences with the same meanings. Sentences are often said to express propositions, for this book no distinction is made between expressing a proposition and making a

---

[1]It may also be thought that the sentence "Snow is white" does contain the embedded sentence "Snow", but we are not taking something non-declarative like "Snow" to be a sentence. It is possible for a noun on its own to carry some meaning, indeed, insofar as a solitary noun may extend proudly from one full-stop to the other it is possible for it to be a sentence. However such sentences are ignored for the porposes of this book.

[2]Note that there is a reading of "that" such that "Jane said that" is declarative, but that reading is not that of "Jane said that grass green...".

statement. Only sentences that make statements (or express propositions) can be true or false.

Thus questions and commands cannot take truth values and therefore are ignored by the logic (propositional logic).

Is grass green?
Open the door!

These sentences do not take truth values.

Let us abbreviate truth to the letter T and falsity to the letter F.[3] So if we mark a particular sentence with a T we mean to say that it is true; if we mark it with an F we mean to say that it is false.

The reason propositional logic is also called *truth-functional* Logic is that a major constituent of it are truth functions. Consider a sentence like "It is not the case that snow is white." We can pick out the embedded sentence and see that what truth value that takes affects the truth of the entire sentence:

"It is not the case that snow is white" is a false sentence.

Or to avoid any dispute involving dirty snow let us use a slightly different embedded sentence:

It is not the case that $1 + 1 = 2$

This is a false sentence by virtue of the fact that the sentence "$1 + 1 = 2$" is a true sentence. We can change the embedded sentence so that the entire sentence becomes true.

It is not the case that black is white.

This sentence is true by virtue of the fact that black is not white.

2.2 Truth values of complex sentences

It is not just embedded sentences that do all the work as far as the truth or falsity of the sentence goes. The non-embedded part – the "It is not the case that" part of the sentence "It is not the case that black is white" – does have something to do with whether the whole sentence is true or false.

The non-embedded parts of a sentence are not meaningful by themselves (as sentences) and so they cannot take truth values.[4] However they do affect the truth value of any sentence that includes them.

Definition 2.2.1 *We say a sentence is* truth functional *when it is impossible to change its truth value (whichever it is of true or false) by changing any main embedded sentence it has for one of the same truth value.*

---

[3]Sometimes you will see True and False to be abbreviated to $\top$ and $\bot$ respectively. $\top$ and $\bot$ are also often used to denote the abstract mathematical objects Truth and Falsity.

[4]This does depend on what your theory of meaning is. Once again for the purposes of this book let us assume that something like "it is not the case that" or "and" is not meaningful as a sentence.

Definition 2.2.2 *In a truth functional sentence the non-embedded parts are called* truth functions.

2.2.1   Truth functional sentences

Consider the already familiar sentence with the (main) embedded sentence underlined:

It is not the case that <u>snow is white</u>

T (true)

The embedded sentence is true so the entire sentence is false:

It is not the case that <u>snow is white</u>

(false) F   T (true)

Let us now start changing the embedded sentence for ones of the same truth value:

It is not the case that <u>Muswell Hill is in England</u>

F   T

There has been no change in the overall truth value.

It is not the case that <u>$1 + 1 = 2$</u>

F   T

Supposing the embedded sentences are false:

It is not the case that <u>Tel Aviv is in England</u>

T   F

If we change the embedded sentence for another false one the entire sentence remains true.

It is not the case that <u>the earth is flat</u>

T   F

There is still no change in the truth value of the entire sentence. If the embedded sentence are true the entire sentence remains false. If the embedded sentences are false the whole sentence remains true. It seems that the sentence "It is not the case that snow is white" is truth functional and because of this the non-embedded part, "It is not the case that," is a truth function. That means that any sentence of the form "It is not the case that..." is truth functional. Let us look at another type of sentence that uses a connective:[5]

---

[5]A connective is a phrase (collection of symbols) that connects sentences together to form new sentences. Some connectives like "it is not the case that" only connect one sentence. Others, like "and" or "or," connect more than one sentence.

Snow is white and grass is green

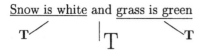

There are two embedded sentences, and the entire sentence is true. Let us now start changing the embedded sentences for ones of the same truth value and see what happens:

Snow is white and $1 + 1 = 2$

The sentence as a whole is still true.

Water is wet and $1 + 1 = 2$

The sentence is still true. What if both the embedded sentences are false?

The earth is flat and Elvis is dead

Here both the embedded sentences are false[6] and so is the entire sentence.

The earth is flat and $1 + 1 = 3$

The sentence is still false.

Fish cannot swim and $1 + 1 = 3$

The embedded sentences are both false and so is the entire sentence. Now see what happens if the embedded sentences have different truth values:

Heretics should be burned and Jimi can sing

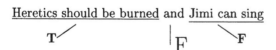

The sentence is false.

Toast should be burnt and Bob Dylan can sing

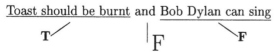

Again the sentence is false. So it seems that no matter what combination of true and false embedded sentences we use it is impossible to change the truth value of the overall sentence by changing the embedded sentences for ones of the same truth value. Any sentence of the form "...and..." is truth functional; hence the connective "and" is a truth function.

---

[6]The King lives.

2.2.2   Non-truth functional sentences

What about non-truth functional sentences? Here is a sentence that is not truth functional.

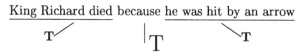

If you are not happy with "he was hit by an arrow" as a proper meaningful embedded sentence, we can rewrite it like this.

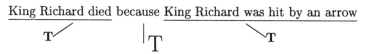

Now we have the two embedded sentences "King Richard died" and "King Richard was hit by an arrow" and the connective "because." The two embedded sentences are true and the whole sentence is true. Now see what happens when we substitute the embedded sentences for ones of the same truth value.

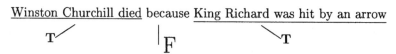

This is clearly false. It is even false if we use the original embedded sentence.

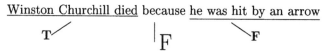

For the connective "because", changing the connected sentences can change the truth value of the overall sentence. All we need is to find one example where this happens in order to know that "because" is not a truth function as a truth function needs to work for all sentences. Here is another sentence which is not truth functional:

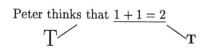

Peter is a mathematical man.

$$\text{Peter thinks that } \underline{\text{in ZF every set is equipollent to an ordinal}}$$
$$F \diagup \qquad\qquad\qquad \diagdown T$$

Peter is not that mathematical.[7] We can change the embedded sentence for another that has the same truth value and change the truth value of the entire

---

[7] In ZF set theory every set is equipollent to an ordinal. However Peter opted not to take the elementary set theory course lest all his friends think him a geek. As a result Peter does not think very much.

sentence. Clearly the non-embedded part of the sentence is not a truth function. This is the difference between an *intensional* sentence and an *extensional* sentence (the "s" is deliberate here). Examples of intensional sentences are "Peter believes X" or "Peter judges X." Example of extensional sentences are "It is not the case that X" or "both X and Y," the intensional sentence are never truth functional.

2.2.3   Different words, same truth function

Jane worked hard but failed her exams

Once again, this may be rewritten as

Jane worked hard but Jane failed her exams

If we assume that the two embedded sentences are true, it seems that the entire sentence is true as well.

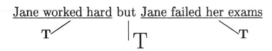

Let us change the sentences about and see what happens.

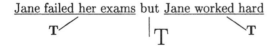

Still true.

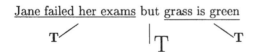

A little unusual but still true.

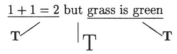

Very unusual but still true. Not only does it seem that "but" is truth functional it also seems that "but" is the same as "and." The only difference between "but" and "and" is that the use of "but" suggests that the second embedded sentence is not what is most naturally expected. However, since this surprise element has no effect on the truth values of any of the embedded sentences or the sentence as a whole the connective "but" is a truth function. Moreover, whenever we see a "but" we can switch it for an "and" and it will make no difference, this suggests that "but" and "and" are in fact the same truth function.

Although Jane worked hard, Jane failed her exams

"Although" looks remarkably like the connective "but" in that it also implies some surprise element in the second embedded sentence. It is also like "but" and "and" in that it is truth functional. You can use the truth function "and" instead of "although":

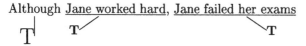

Although <u>Jane worked hard, Jane failed her exams</u>

We can change the embedded sentences, and the truth value of the entire sentence does not change.

Although <u>1 + 1 = 2, the Earth is round</u>

A little strange, but still true. It can be seen quite easily that truth functions like "although" and "despite the fact that" behave just like "and." There is a more interesting contender to be a truth function, the connective "or" which can be written "either...or."

2.2.4 Same word, different truth functions

Either <u>Peter went to the party</u> or <u>Jane went to the party</u>

If only one of the two embedded sentences is true – Peter did go to the party and Jane did not – then clearly the whole sentence is true. It is true that either Peter went or Jane went,

Either <u>Peter went to the party</u> or <u>Jane went to the party</u>

If we change the sentences there is no difference to the truth value of the sentence.

Either <u>1 + 1 = 2</u> or <u>the Earth is flat</u>

It is not everyday that you come across a sentence like this. However if you ignore its weirdness, it is true. Most of the following sentences seem very weird in that a little relevance is expected between the two embedded sentences. Truth functions are only concerned with the truth values of the sentences and ignore any implied causal links or relevance between the sentences. Remember not to expect any relevance or link between the two embedded sentences. Because 1 + 1 = 2, it is true that either 1 + 1 = 2 or the Earth is flat. So "or" looks like a truth function.

Either <u>2 + 2 = 5</u> or <u>Snow is white</u>

This is also true and looks remarkably similar to the last sentence, just the other way round. That is, the embedded sentence on the left is now the false one, while the embedded sentence on the right is now the true one.

Let us try changing the embedded sentences for ones of the same truth values:

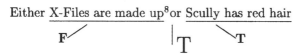

Either X-Files are made up[8] or Scully has red hair
F | T | T

The sentence is still true; by virtue of Dana Scully having red hair it is true that either the X-Files are made up or Scully has red hair. "Or" looks even more truth functional.

Either pigs can fly or London is in France
F | F | F

Both the embedded sentences are false and the whole sentence is also false. Here is a slightly more intuitive example that also shows the sentence to be truth functional.

Either the earth is absolutely flat or the earth is a big cube
F | F | F

This sentence is clearly false since the Earth is round. Now see what happens if both the embedded sentences are true.

Either $1 + 1 = 2$ or $3 + 3 = 6$
T | T | T

It seems that this statement is true, but imagine this scenario. Supposing you are in a restaurant and you ask the waiter what you can have in your soup and he says:

Either one can have dumplings or one can have croutons

A little later you see the waiter serve a rather fat man in the corner with both dumplings and croutons. Naturally you feel a little annoyed and instantly call the waiter over to give him an earful for leading you to believe that you could not have both. Suppose the waiter really did mean that one could not have both, then what he said was false if both its embedded sentences turn out to be true:

Either one can have dumplings or one can have croutons
T | F | T

---

[8]The FBI cannot openly admit to the truth of the X-Files but they have a duty to the truth. So they release the files in film, as a drama. No, really.

This is not the end of the matter. Consider the next scenario. You are at a bus stop and you ask a man waiting there what the next bus will be. He replies:

Either <u>A number 43 bus will come</u> or <u>A number 134 bus will come</u>"

Typically you wait around for ages and then both a number 43 and a 134 bus turn up. It would be considered very strange indeed to turn to the man and say "you lied to me, they both came!" It seems from this that both the embedded sentences are true and so is the entire sentence.

Either <u>A number 43 bus will come</u> or <u>A number 134 bus will come</u>

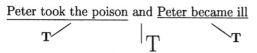

There is something going on here: it would be very useful if "or" was in fact a truth function but this problem which cannot be put down to a glitch in the use of English. We shall say that it is not a problem of one truth function, but of two truth functions getting mixed up. There is the *exclusive* "or" for which when both the embedded sentences are true the whole sentence is false. There is also the *inclusive* "or" for which when both the embedded sentences are true the entire sentence is true.

The Englsh language lost the distinction between the inclusive and exclusive "or"; "aut...aut" and "vel...vel" existed in Latin. In English you can sometimes tell the difference between the two by looking at the context in which the sentence is used. As a matter of fact, the ambiguity can get so nasty that in legal documents they use the term "and/or" to signify the inclusive "or" and something like "but not both" when they use the exclusive "or".

2.3   A problem for truth functionality

There are some problems with our truth functions as interpretations of English words. Sometimes they can be used when slightly different connectives are really meant. Consider the following sentence:

<u>Peter took the poison</u> and <u>Peter became ill</u>

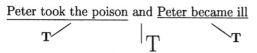

Let us assume these truth values are the correct ones. Now here is a way of changing the embedded sentences for ones of the same truth value without thinking of any new sentences.

<u>Peter became ill</u> and <u>Peter became ill</u>

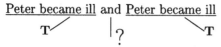

Is this sentence true or false? Does it have the same meaning as the one before it? The ambiguity here is that the "and" could be taken in both sentences to mean "and then." That way the sentence "Peter became ill and then Peter took the poison" becomes false because it is true that Peter took the poison first: "Peter took the poison and then Peter became ill." There is argument here as to whether this is a general problem. Some philosophers think that this a genuine case where the connective "and" is not truth functional because of this temporal quality. Others will say that it is not a problem at all, since the sentence "Peter became ill and Peter took the poison" is true if the sentence "Peter took the poison and Peter became ill" is true. Others admit a pragmatic problem about the use of "and" but maintain its truth functionality. We shall take "and" as truth functional and ignore cases such as this.

There is another connective that can be very problematic, the infamous "if...then...." In natural language it appears to have many complex meanings so that many agree that it is not in fact a truth function. However, others say that it is a truth function and people use it badly and expect too much of it. Propositional logic contains a truth function (which we shall deal with later) that some believe provides a correct analysis of "if...then...." Such sentences are a very important piece of natural language, and any logic that attempts to analyze natural language would be almost useless if it could not deal with them. It would be pointless to go into the nature of "if...then..." sentences (called *conditionals*) here as people have been writing entire books on the subject ever since the dawn of time.[9] For the moment just accept that "if...then..." is a truth function; whenever you can rewrite a sentence using "if...then...," take that sentence to be truth functional (the truth function being "if...then..."). We shall discuss the conditional and look at its logic in more detail in Chapter 5.

2.4 Exercises

State which of the following underlined expressions (which may be split over the sentence) are truth functions. Where you have decided that the expression is not a truthfunction, show that it is not.

1. It is false that snow is white.

2. The politician hopes that the photographs will not be released.

3. Unless there is rain, the match will be played.

4. The match will be played until there is rain.

5. Although it rained the match was played.

6. It is possible that it snowed yesterday.

7. Is it the case that the election was rigged?

8. Make sure that the door is closed.

9. Neither will it rain nor will it snow.

---

[9]Look in any philosophy/logic library for books with the word "counterfactuals" in the title and see how many of them there are.

10. <u>It is self-evident that</u> $1 + 1 = 2$.

Chapter 3

Formalisation of Truth Functions

3.1 Formalising truth functions

3.1.1 Formalising *and*, *not*, and *or*

We want our logic to be a formal system. That means we want a simple way to use universal language for our logic to operate in. We also want to provide some solid definitions of the way our logic works. The most important part of our logic are truth functions. We shall denote them with symbols to allow for greater control, rigour and ease. Unfortunately there is no standard set of symbols to use (so much for universal); however, there are not that many variants and all good logic books specify at the start what all their symbols mean.

Truth Function	Possible Symbols
And/*Conjunction*	∧ · &
It is not the case that (Not)/*Negation*	¬ ~
Or (inclusive)/*Disjunction*	∨
Or (exclusive)	no official symbol

So whenever we see an "and," a "but," a "not," or an "or," we can substitute the appropriate symbol for it. The symbols we shall use in this book are as follows:

Definition 3.1.1

Truth Function	My Symbols
And	·
Negation	~
Or (inclusive)	∨

It is generally a good idea to read the symbols as if they were words; that way, seeing and using them becomes more natural and easy. So whenever you see a "." read it as "and," a "∨" is "or" and a "∼" (tilde) may be read as "not" or "it is not the case that. . . ."

Definition 3.1.2 *From now on whenever the word "or" is used it is the* inclusive *"or," unless specified otherwise.*

3.1.2   Formalising sentences

We use capital letters taken from the start of the alphabet to symbolize sentences or statements (some books will use letters from the middle of the alphabet, occasionally not capital.[1]) Because of this we do not have to keep rewriting the sentence each time we want to express it. Provided we specify which letters denote which sentence, we can express much information with just a few symbols. Let us now formalize a few sentences:

It is not the case that it is raining can be formalized like this:

Key $\sim A$

A = It is raining

The key is very important because it tells anyone reading the sentence $\sim A$ what the A part means (he should know that the $\sim$ part means "it is not the case that").

Oranges are sticky and Carbon is black

Key $A \cdot B$

A = Oranges are sticky
B = Carbon is black

Either I'll get a bus or I'll get a taxi

Key $A \vee B$

A = I'll get a bus
B = I'll get a taxi

In this case the "or" might be thought of as being exclusive, but it also has an inclusive reading. We shall take the inclusive reading of disjunctions and formalise them with ∨.[2]

---

[1]There are not that many different notation conventions; however, you will find many books that use symbols like p, q and r to refer to sentences and symbols like A, B and C to refer to other things. Occasionally you will find people using Greek lettering, α, β. Make sure you know exactly what notation convention they is using when someone start throwing symbols at you.

[2]see page 42 and Section 4.3 for a way of formalising exclusive disjunctions.

Suppose we have the sentence, **Snow is not white**. We can formalize it like this:

Key	$\underline{A}$
A = Snow is not white	

Actually, we could have formalized all the previous sentences as one letter. So we could have reduced "Oranges are sticky and carbon is black" to the statement A but this more or less defeats the purpose of everything we are doing.

Here is a second way. **Snow is not white** has exactly the truth conditions of **It is not the case the snow is white**, so we can just substitute one for the other and then formalize the new one.

Key	$\sim A$
A = Snow is white	

The second is the more useful formalisation as it contains more logical information. As a general rule, the more truth functions and distinct sentences you can turn a sentence into the better, because you can show more arguments to be valid. It must be stressed that writing "Snow is not white" as A is not wrong, it is just *unhelpful*.

If you have a sentence that contains more than one truth function, you can separate the truth functions with parentheses to avoid any confusion as to which sentence applies to which truth function. Suppose we have the sentence **Grass is green and it is not the case that snow is black**. We can formalize it like this:

Key	$A \cdot \sim B$
A = Grass is green	
B = Snow is black	

There is no chance of misreading this formalisation, but suppose we had decided to write the sentence the other way round: **It is not the case that snow is black and grass is green**.

Key	$\sim A \cdot B$
A = Snow is black	
B = Grass is green	

This sentence seems to be translatable back into natural language in two different ways, one of which does not retain the sentence's original meaning.

1. **It is not the case that snow is black, and grass is green.** The intended way.

2. **It is not the case that, [both] snow is black and grass is green.** Not what is intended.

We can get around this problem by using brackets:

1. Key $(\sim A) \cdot B$
    A = Snow is black
    B = Grass is green

2. Key $\sim(A \cdot B)$
    A = Snow is black
    B = Grass is green

There is clearly a difference between the two. Let us formalize some more sentences.

It is not the case that I am either intelligent or stupid.

This sentence splits up like this:

It is not the case that (I am either intelligent or stupid).

We can rewrite the sentence inside the brackets in a much easier form so we get:

It is not the case that (either I am intelligent or I am stupid).

This formalizes very nicely like this:

Key $\sim(A \vee B)$
A = I am intelligent
B = I am stupid

Either it is not raining or both Peter and Jane are wet.

First we will need some way to split this up. It seems to split up like this:

Either (it is not raining) or (both Peter and Jane are wet).

The sentences inside the brackets can split up further:

Either (it is not the case that it is raining) or ((Peter is wet) and (Jane is wet)).

This sentence formalizes quite easily now:

Key $(\sim A) \vee (B \cdot C)$
A = It is raining
B = Peter is wet
C = Jane is wet

The formalized sentence is much, much simpler and is far easier to see all at once.

Elvis is not dead and he is living in the Bermuda Triangle

We can rewrite this as "Elvis is not dead and Elvis is living in the Bermuda Triangle" then it can be rewritten like this:

Elvis is not dead...

It is not the case that Elvis is dead and Elvis is living in the Bermuda Triangle

and...

he is living in the Bermuda Triangle.

It then formalizes very easily:

Key $\qquad\qquad (\sim A) \cdot B$
$\overline{A}$ = Elvis is dead
B = Elvis is living in the Bermuda Triangle

Either Shergar is dead or he is not and is living with Elvis

Can be taken to mean one of two things:

1.   Either Shergar is dead...

Either Shergar is dead or ((it is not the case that Shergar is dead) and (Shergar is living with Elvis))

or he is not and is living with Elvis.

2.   Either Shergar is dead or he is not...

(Either (Shergar is dead) or (it is not the case that Shergar is dead)) and Shergar is living with Elvis

and [whichever he is]
he is living with Elvis.

This is an example of an ambiguous sentence; there are two possibilities for what it could mean. The first says that either Shergar is dead and, if he is not dead that he is living with Elvis. The second says that either Shergar is dead or he is not and, regardless of whether he is dead or not, he is living with Elvis (in horsie and rock'n'roll heaven for example). Despite (1) seeming to be more plausible than (2), both have some meaning. Some more information is needed in order to decide which one to use. Formalising both makes the difference between them clearer:

Key $\qquad\qquad A \vee [\, (\sim A) \cdot B \,]$
1. $\overline{A}$ = Shergar is dead
B = Shergar is living with Elvis

Key $\qquad\qquad [\, A \vee (\sim A) \,] \cdot B$
2. $\overline{A}$ = Shergar is dead
B = Shergar is living with Elvis

On with the examples:

Either Peter or Jane is going to the party but not both

We can split this up like this:

> **(Either Peter is going to the party or Jane is going to the party) and (it is not the case that [Peter is going to the party and Jane is going to the party[3]])**

This then can be formalized using only two sentences:

Key
A = Peter is going to the party
B = Jane is going to the party

$$(A \lor B) \cdot \sim(A \cdot B)$$

What we have said here is that either A or B but not both. This is the exclusive "or"; it has been defined in terms of $\cdot$ (and), $\sim$ (Not) and $\lor$ (Or).

It is not the case that Peter is not intelligent

This really does not need to be rewritten, but it can be:

> **It is not the case that (it is not the case that Peter is intelligent)**

The formalisation for this double negative is exactly that.

Key
A = Peter is intelligent

$$\sim(\sim A)$$

It should be easy to see that the brackets are not required. We could have saved ink and done the following:

Key
A = Peter is intelligent

$$\sim \sim A$$

Later on we shall show, with our logic, that the sentence $\sim \sim A$ has the same *truth conditions* as A. The truth conditions are the conditions by which a sentence is true; if two sentences have the same truth conditions, then there is no way one can be true while the other is false.

The music is neither loud nor annoying

This means that the music is not loud, it is not annoying and it is not both loud and annoying. So we can rewrite the sentence like this:

> **It is not the case that (the music is loud) and it is not the case that (the music is annoying).**

This now formalizes in the usual way.

Key
A = The music is loud
B = The music is annoying

$$\sim A \cdot \sim B$$

We could also have read the sentence in a different way.

---

[3]Do not loose sleep over this sentence's apparent complexity.

It is not the case that (the music is loud or annoying)

Of course this can then be rewritten like this:

It is not the case that (either (the music is loud) or (the music is annoying))

We can now formalize this easily.

Key $\sim(A \lor B)$
$A = $ The music is loud
$B = $ The music is annoying

It should be clear that the two formalisations are both accurate.

3.2 Truth Tables

3.2.1 How to read truth tables

Now that we have devised a system by which we can formalize sentences of natural language, we should devise a system by which we can do some logic on them. The important parts of our logic system so far are the truth functions; as their name suggests, they are the main operators of the logic, and do all the work. Earlier we said truth functions operate independently of the meanings of the sentences they connect or are attached to. The truth functions are dependent entirely on the truth *values* of the sentences they are attached to. We should devise a system by which we can determine the truth values of entire sentences just from knowing the truth values of the embedded sentences and the truth functions involved. The most intuitive system for doing this is using *Truth Tables*. If you have done any electronics you may already have met truth tables for circuit gates; the general ideas behind them are similar to those used in logic. A truth table is a simple way of displaying all possible cases and determining what happens in each case.

3.2.2 Negation

Here is the truth table for negation (tilde or $\sim$):

Definition 3.2.1

$\sim$	A
F	T
T	F

Possible truth values of the sentence A. A could be any sentence, a simple one or one involving many truth functions.[4]

Truth values of sentence $\sim A$ given the truth values of A.

---

[4]To understand the truth table see that A and B can each be either true or false. But there are four ways this can happen:

1. both are true

2. A is true and B is false

- Look under the heading **A**: there are two truth values there. These are the possible truth values that sentence A could take (it does not matter what sentence A is just as long as it is a sentence).

- For each truth value under **A** there is a corresponding truth value under (the heading) $\sim$; this is the truth value that the sentence $\sim A$ would take. So if the sentence A is true, then the sentence $\sim A$ is false; if the sentence A is false then the sentence $\sim A$ is true.

- This is intuitive. The sentence "Snow is white" is True, so the sentence "It is not the case that snow is white" is false.

- The sentence "Grass is pink" is false, so the sentence "It is not the case that grass is pink" must be true.

- Looking at the truth table for negation we see that all it does is reverse the truth value of the sentence to which it is attached. If a sentence A is true then the sentence $\sim A$ will be false, if A is false, then $\sim A$ will be true. So if the more complex sentence $A \cdot B$ is true, then the sentence $\sim(A \cdot B)$ is false, etc.

3.2.3 Conjunction

Here is the truth table for $\cdot$.

Definition 3.2.2

$\cdot$	A	B
T	T	T
F	T	F
F	F	T
F	F	F

All possible combinations For the truth values of the sentences A and B.

Truth values of sentence $A \cdot B$ given the truth values of A and B.

- According to this table the sentence $A \cdot B$ is true when the embedded sentences A and B are true.

- If one or both of the embedded sentences are false, then the whole sentence $A \cdot B$ is false. "The sun is shining and the sky is blue" is false when either the sun is not shining or the sky is not blue (or both).

- When the sentences A and B are true the sentence $A \cdot B$ is true and because we are dealing with truth functions here it does not matter what the embedded sentences A and B mean (just as long as they can take truth values, i.e. be true or false).

---

3. A is false and B is true

4. both are false

each of which is expressed by the columns on the right. The left column indicates the truth or falsity of the whole sentence $A \cdot B$ for each combination. So for example the top row tells us that $A \cdot B$ is true when both A and B are true.

The truth table for ∨ (Or) should have the same number of rows and columns the truth table for · (and), because they are both connectives for two sentences.

3.2.4 Disjunction

Definition 3.2.3

∨	A	B
T	T	T
T	T	F
T	F	T
F	F	F

All possible combinations
For the truth values of the
sentences A and B.

Truth values of sentence $A \lor B$
given the truth values of A and B.

- The Ts and Fs in the **A** and **B** columns are exactly the same in the table for "·" and the table for ∨. That order of Ts and Fs is the standard way of representing the four possible cases involving the sentences A and B. A and B can both be true, they can both be false, and there are two ways one can be false while the other is true (either A is false and B is true or A is true and B is false). It is merely a convention that the truth values in the **A** column and **B** column are written out in this particular order.

- According to the truth table, if both the embedded sentences A and B are true then the entire sentence is true.

- The truth table also states that if one of the embedded sentences is true, then the whole sentence is also true (this is from the second and third lines of the truth table).

- Finally the truth table says that if both the embedded sentences are false, then the entire sentence is also false. So for the sentence $A \lor B$ to be true we must have at least one of the two embedded sentences A and B being true; otherwise the sentence is false.

3.3 Material equivalence

3.3.1 The formalisation of material equivalence

There is another truth function which we shall now discuss before we go on to some logical operations. There seems to be no specific phrase of natural language equivalent to this truth function. This does not mean that we never use it in natural language, it is just that it tends to be implied rather than stated explicitly.[5] This truth function is called *material equivalence* and its natural language equivalents are "...has the same truth value as..." or "...if

---

[5]It is to the great annoyance of many that much of the time we use the connective "if ...then..." to mean "...if and only if..." or "...is equivalent to...."

and only if...."[6] It is much easier however to read this truth function as "...has the same truth value as...." Note that the WRONG way of reading material equivalence is "...is the same as saying..." or "...means..."; these sorts of connective mean something related but considerably different.

Note the distinction between material equivalence and logical equivalence. If "A is materially equivalent to B" is true, then A and B just happen to have the same truth values. If "A is logically equivalent to B" is true, then A and B always have the same truth values, no matter what.

This truth function also has many commonly used symbols:

Truth Function	Possible Symbols
Material equivalence	$\Leftrightarrow \equiv \leftrightarrow$

The symbol we shall adopt is the triple lined equal sign $\equiv$ (called the *congruence symbol*).

It is important to remember that material equivalence is *not* the same as the Symbol = (equals). The equals symbol represents a relation between objects, the relation is *identity*, the congruence symbol represents a relation between the truth values of sentences. So $x = y$ means that x and y are the same thing, $A \equiv B$ means that A and B have the same truth value this clearly does not mean that A and B have to be the same.[7] The fact that $\equiv$ and = look similar can be confusing but it must be made clear that the two are nothing like each other.

Definition 3.3.1

Truth Function	*My Symbol*
Material equivalence	$\equiv$

Let us look at the truth table for material equivalence.

Definition 3.3.2

$\equiv$	A	B
T	T	T
F	T	F
F	F	T
T	F	F

3.3.2   Material equivalence in sentences

As we can see from Def 3.3.2, the sentence $A \equiv B$ is true only when both the embedded sentences have the same truth value (the first and the last rows), this

---

[6]Often "A if and only if B" is used to assert some necessary connection between A and B rather than the weaker statement that they have the same truth value. In such a use of "if and only if" it would be incorrect to formalize it as material equivalence.

[7]$A = B$ would mean, if anything, that A and B are the *same sentence*, i.e. using identical words.

is why we can read the truth function as "...has the same truth value as...."
This is an important and useful truth function.

Just to emphasise an earlier a point, here is a difference between equality and material equivalence:

Peter's mind = Peter's brain.

This sentence states highly argued claim – that a person's mind *is identical with* his brain. Contrast this doctrine with:

Jane has a mind ≡ Jane has a brain.

The above sentence says that the two sentences "Jane has a mind" and "Jane has a brain" have the same truth values. This means that it is not true that Jane has a brain and no mind or that she has a mind and no brain. This does not entail that Jane's mind and Jane's brain are the same object.[8]

3.4 Exercises

Translate the following sentences into formal logic using letters (A, B, C) for sentences and ∼, ·, and ∨ for the appropriate truth-functions.

1. John did not go to the cinema.

2. Either John went to the cinema or he went to the party.

3. Either Mary likes John and she likes David or she is lying.

4. John went to the party but Jane did not.

5. Although Jane went to the party John did not.

6. John likes Jane or he doesn't.

7. It is not the case that John doesn't like Jane.

The following sentences are ambiguous. Translate each one two ways into formal logic using letters (A, B, C) for sentences and ∼ , ·, and ∨ for the appropriate truth-functions.

8. It is not the case that Jane went to the cinema and John stayed in.

9. Either John went to the cinema or Jane stayed in and Mary stayed in.

---

[8]Remember that "Jane has a mind ≡ Jane has a brain" states that the two embedded sentences just *happen* to have the same truth value. More interesting is a sentence like "Necessarily, Jane has a mind ≡ Jane has a brain."

Chapter 4

Truth Tables and Tautologies

4.1 Tautologies and how to find them

We are now equipped with enough machinery to do some logical operations. We can use our truth tables to analyze some abstract sentences (sentences written in propositional logic without any meaning specified for the sentences involved, i.e. sentences without a key) and see if they are tautologies.

Definition 4.1.1 *A sentence is a tautology when no matter what truth values its embedded sentences take it always takes the truth value T (true). Only propositions that cannot be false in propositional logic may be called tautologies.*

Fact 4.1.2 *A sentence is a tautology when the column under the main connective of its truth table does not contain an F.*

Note that there is a distinction between "tautology" and "logical necessity." A logical necessity is a sentence that must be true given our logical understanding of its terms. A tautology is a sentence that must be true only because of its truth functional structure.[1] All tautologies are logical necessities but not all logical necessities are tautologies. For example, "If not everyone is listening then someone is not listening" is logically necessary, but not only because of the truth function "if... then... "; the understanding of "everyone" and "someone" plays a key role as well.

An example of a tautology is the sentence "grass is blue or grass is not blue." Notice that it must be true, but not because of the meanings of "grass" and "blue"; any sentence expressing that something is the case or it is not, must be true. This distinction should become clearer as the book progresses. A sentence is a tautology when it can be shown to be necessarily true using *only* propositional logic (see Def 4.1.1).

---

[1]Or, it must be true only on our logical understanding of its truth functions.

All that we need now is some method by which we can determine whether a sentence is a tautology or not. We can do this quite easily using truth tables. Let us begin with the simple sentence:

$$A \vee \sim A$$

This sentence says that either A or not A, it may be easier to read this as either sentence A is true or sentence A is not true.[2] This is not saying much and is intuitively quite obvious. Here is how the truth tables prove that it is a tautology.

First, write a list of all the possible truth values underneath the sentences that are denoted by letters (as we did in the truth tables earlier). Because there is only one letter used in this sentence there is only one possible combination. Also, even though the letter is used twice, the list should be the same under both letters. If any letter is used more than once in the same sentence when you list its possible truth values, the lists must be the same under the same letter.

$$
\begin{array}{cccc}
A & \vee & \sim & A \\
T & & & T \\
F & & & F
\end{array}
$$

In English, A is either true or it is false.[3] If the A on the left hand side is true then the A on the right hand side must also be true, and likewise if it is false. Now the question arises: what truth values do we fill in next, the $\vee$ or the $\cdot$? To answer this we introduce a bit of jargon. This sentence has two embedded sentences, the sentence A and the sentence $\sim A$, one of these sentences has an embedded sentence itself. If we look at the sentence as a whole we see that the truth function for the entire sentence is the $\vee$, this truth function is called the *main connective*. If we really over-bracket the entire sentence like this:

$$(A) \vee (\sim(A))$$

then the truth function that is outside all the brackets is the main connective.

Definition 4.1.3 *The main connective of a sentence is the truth function which is outside all the brackets. The main connective need not connect two sentences, it could be a negation symbol*

The main connective is the one we fill in last, this is because its truth value depends on the sentences it connects (with negation there is only one) and so they should be determined first. As a matter of fact, this gives us an easy way to determine in which order to fill the possible truth values. Start with the truth functions with the most brackets around them and work your way out. Fill in the possible truth values for the sentences that are denoted by letters

---

[2]It is a good formalisation of the sentence "grass is blue or it is not".

[3]Notice that the necessity of $A \vee \sim A$, that A is either true or false, is in a sense assumed when we only write down only two possible truth values for A in the truth table: true and false. Please ignore this apparent circularity (see footnote, 99)

(write the Ts and the Fs under the letters first), then fill in the possible truth values for the ones with the most brackets around them. Remember that the negation symbols have unwritten brackets around them, which we omit to avoid a bracket overload. However, imagine they are there for the purposes of filling out the Ts and the Fs. Therefore we fill in the $\sim$ column before the $\lor$ column in the above example, since the $\sim$ has more brackets around it (the $\lor$ being the main connective has no brackets around it). We fill in the negation by looking at the truth value of the sentence it is operating on and then looking at its truth table to see what value it takes. To form the truth table of negation we see that it reverses the truth values of the sentence it operates on. In this example the sentence it operates on is A.

$$
\begin{array}{ccc}
A & \lor & \sim & A \\
T & & \mathbf{F} & T \\
F & & \mathbf{T} & F
\end{array}
$$

What we are stating here is the possible truth values for the sentences A and $\sim A$. So if the sentence A on the left is true the sentence $\sim A$ (look under the negation sign) is false and if the sentence A on the left is false the sentence $\sim A$ is true. Now there is only one column left; we fill that in using the truth values of the sentences it connects (the truth values of the sentences A and $\sim A$). Looking at the truth table for $\lor$ we see that any sentence of the form $A \lor B$ is true when at least one of the sentences it connects is true, otherwise it is false. In the first row of the example one of the sentences around the $\lor$ is true – namely the sentence A – on the left, so in the first row the $\lor$ is true:

$$
\begin{array}{cccc}
A & \lor & \sim & A \\
T & \mathbf{T} & F & T \\
F & & T & F
\end{array}
$$

We see also that in the second column that at least one of the two sentences around the $\lor$ is true, namely the sentence $\sim A$ on the right, so in the second row the $\lor$ takes the value true:

$$
\begin{array}{cccc}
A & \lor & \sim & A \\
T & T & F & T \\
F & \mathbf{T} & T & F
\end{array}
$$

Now, from this table, we see that no matter what truth values the sentence A takes, the main connective of the sentence $A \lor \sim A$ takes the value true.

Definition 4.1.4 *The truth value of an entire truth functional sentence is the truth value of the main connective.*

No matter what the embedded sentences of the sentence $A \lor \sim A$ are, the entire sentence is true. We have just proved our first tautology. This sentence is called the *law of excluded middle* – something is either true or false, there is no in-between truth value. Let us try another sentence.

$$\sim(A \cdot \sim A)$$

Here the main connective (a connective does not have to connect two sentences, it may operate only on one) is the negation sign on the far left, which is outside all the brackets. We start by filling in the possible truth values for the sentence A.

$$
\begin{array}{ccccc}
\sim & (A & \cdot & \sim & A) \\
 & T & & & T \\
 & F & & & F \\
\end{array}
$$

Next we do the truth function that is enclosed in the most brackets. Remembering that there are unwritten brackets around the negation sign, we see that the next truth function to fill in is the negation next to the A on the right:

$$
\begin{array}{ccccc}
\sim & (A & \cdot & \sim & A) \\
 & T & & \mathbf{F} & T \\
 & F & \cdot & \mathbf{T} & F \\
\end{array}
$$

The next truth function to fill in is the $\cdot$ as it has more brackets around it than all the other truth functions that are left (namely the negation which is the main connective anyway). From the truth table for $\cdot$ we see that it is true when the two sentences around it are both true, and otherwise it is false. The two sentences around the $\cdot$ here are of course the sentences A and $\sim A$. The sentence itself expresses the classic contradiction, so we would expect the truth values for the $\cdot$ to come out as all false, this is exactly what happens. In the first row it is not the case that both sentences are true as the sentence $\sim A$ has the value false.

$$
\begin{array}{ccccc}
\sim & (A & \cdot & \sim & A) \\
 & T & \mathbf{F} & F & T \\
 & F & & T & F \\
\end{array}
$$

In the second row it is also not the case that both sentences are true. The sentence A is false, so the $\cdot$ is false also.

$$
\begin{array}{ccccc}
\sim & (A & \cdot & \sim & A) \\
 & T & F & F & T \\
 & F & \mathbf{F} & T & F \\
\end{array}
$$

Now the main connective will operate on the main connective of the embedded sentence. If we take the sentence $(A \cdot \sim A)$ with no negation on the far left, we see that the main connective for that is the $\cdot$. This means that the negation in the sentence $\sim(A \cdot \sim A)$ operates on the $\cdot$. We know that negation just reverses the truth values, so we can write down the truth values for the whole sentence.

$$
\begin{array}{ccccc}
\sim & (A & \cdot & \sim & A) \\
\mathbf{T} & T & F & F & T \\
\mathbf{T} & F & F & T & F \\
\end{array}
$$

This sentence, also a tautology is called the *law of non-contradiction*. The law of excluded middle and the law of non-contradiction are very closely related, and since both are tautologies they are in fact logically equivalent (they always take the same truth value, True). They are in fact so similar that some people occasionally make the mistake of referring to them by the same name. Some call them both non-contradiction, or excluded middle. To do this is a logical sin. Non-contradiction and excluded-middle are distinct and should be kept distinct. There are perfectly good logic systems that maintain one and deny the other.

Let us try another sentence:

$$\sim A \lor B$$

The main connective here is the $\lor$. Remember that there are unwritten brackets around the negation: $\sim A$ is short for $(\sim A)$. We write out the possible truth values for the letters, and we want all possible combinations. When there are two letters involved we do it like this:

$\sim$	A	$\lor$	B
	T		T
	T		F
	F		T
	F		F

These are all the possible combinations of T and F for two different sentences. Either they are both true, or one is true and the other is false, or they are both false. The next truth function to deal with is the negation. This just reverses the truth value of the sentence it operates on, the A.

$\sim$	A	$\lor$	B
F	T		T
F	T		F
T	F		T
T	F		F

Now there is only one column left, the one for the $\lor$. Look at the truth values for the two sentences it connects, the sentence $\sim A$ and the sentence B. So we look at the truth values under the B and the truth values under the $\sim$ of $\sim A$. From the truth table for $\lor$ we see that it is true when at least one of the sentences it connects is true, and if both are false then it is also false.

$\sim$	A	$\lor$	B
F	T	**T**	T
F	T	**F**	F
T	F	**T**	T
T	F	**T**	F

We can see that in the second row the sentence is false. This means that if A is true and B is false then the sentence $\sim A \lor B$ is false. It is not a tautology.

Let us look at another sentence.

$$\sim(A \cdot \sim B)$$

The main connective here is the negation on the far left because it is outside all brackets. Once again, we first fill in all the possible truth values for A and B:

$\sim$	$(A$	$\cdot$	$\sim$	$B)$
	T			T
	T			F
	F			T
	F			F

The next truth function to fill in is the negation next to the B as it has the most brackets around it.

$\sim$	$(A$	$\cdot$	$\sim$	$B)$
	T		**F**	T
	T		**T**	F
	F	'	**F**	T
	F		**T**	F

Next we do the $\cdot$ because it is inside a bracket, and the only other column left (the negation on the far left) is not. Remember that the $\cdot$ is true when both the sentences it connects are true. Here the sentences it connects are A and $\sim B$.

$\sim$	$(A$	$\cdot$	$\sim$	$B)$
	T	**F**	F	T
	T	**T**	T	F
	F	**F**	F	T
	F	**F**	T	F

Finally we do the negation. This will reverse the truth values of the main connective of the sentence it is attached to, the $\cdot$ in this case.

$\sim$	$(A$	$\cdot$	$\sim$	$B)$
T	T	F	F	T
F	T	T	T	F
T	F	F	F	T
T	F	F	T	F

For this sentence if A is true and B is false then the entire sentence is false. This sentence is not a tautology.

The two sentences seem to be false only when A is true and B is false, this suggests that they are logically equivalent (always take the same truth values). Let us check this.

$$(\sim A \lor B) \equiv \sim(A \cdot \sim B)$$

The main connective here is the material equivalence symbol, the $\equiv$. However, first we list the possible truth values for all the letters.

$$
\begin{array}{ccccccccc}
(\sim & A & \vee & B) & \equiv & \sim & (A & \cdot & \sim & B) \\
& T & & T & & & T & & & T \\
& T & & F & & & T & & & F \\
& F & & T & & & F & & & T \\
& F & & F & & & F & & & F \\
\end{array}
$$

Next we fill in the negations that are inside the most brackets. Here, since the negation on the A on the left is in one set of brackets and the negation on the B on the right also in one set of brackets, we can do them both together.

$$
\begin{array}{ccccccccc}
(\sim & A & \vee & B) & \equiv & \sim & (A & \cdot & \sim & B) \\
\mathbf{F} & T & & T & & & T & & \mathbf{F} & T \\
\mathbf{F} & T & & F & & & T & & \mathbf{T} & F \\
\mathbf{T} & F & & T & & & F & & \mathbf{F} & T \\
\mathbf{T} & F & & F & & & F & & \mathbf{T} & F \\
\end{array}
$$

The same goes for the $\vee$ and the $\cdot$ that we should do next. Because they are both in one set of brackets, we do them together:

$$
\begin{array}{ccccccccc}
(\sim & A & \vee & B) & \equiv & \sim & (A & \cdot & \sim & B) \\
F & T & \mathbf{T} & T & & & T & \mathbf{F} & F & T \\
F & T & \mathbf{F} & F & & & T & \mathbf{T} & T & F \\
T & F & \mathbf{T} & T & & & F & \mathbf{F} & F & T \\
T & F & \mathbf{T} & F & & & F & \mathbf{F} & T & F \\
\end{array}
$$

The next truth function to do is the negation attached to the sentence $(A \cdot \sim B)$ as this has an unwritten set of brackets around it. Remember it operates on the $\cdot$ as that is the main connective of the sentence inside the brackets (which is the sentence the negation is negating).

$$
\begin{array}{ccccccccc}
(\sim & A & \vee & B) & \equiv & \sim & (A & \cdot & \sim & B) \\
F & T & T & T & & \mathbf{T} & T & F & F & T \\
F & T & F & F & & \mathbf{F} & T & T & T & F \\
T & F & T & T & & \mathbf{T} & F & F & F & T \\
T & F & T & F & & \mathbf{T} & F & F & T & F \\
\end{array}
$$

Now we can fill in the truth values for the material equivalence, looking at the main connectives of each of the embedded sentences. These are the $\vee$ of the first and the $\sim$ of thesecond.

$$
\begin{array}{ccccccccc}
(\sim & A & \vee & B) & \equiv & \sim & (A & \cdot & \sim & B) \\
F & T & T & T & \mathbf{T} & T & T & F & F & T \\
F & T & F & F & \mathbf{T} & F & T & T & T & F \\
T & F & T & T & \mathbf{T} & T & F & F & F & T \\
T & F & T & F & \mathbf{T} & T & F & F & T & F \\
\end{array}
$$

We have shown this sentence to be a tautology. The sentence $\sim A \vee B$ is logically equivalent to the sentence $\sim(A \cdot \sim B)$.

4.2   Truth tables with more than two letters

Here is how we write the Ts and the Fs under the As, Bs, and Cs when only three letters A, B, and C; are used:

A	–	B	–	C
T		T		T
T		T		F
T		F		T
T		F		F
F		T		T
F		T		F
F		F		T
F		F		F

Here is a sentence with three letters representing sentences in it:

$$A \lor B \lor C$$

This sentence is ambiguous; it could be either $A \lor (B \lor C)$ or it could mean $(A \lor B) \lor C$. Let us see what happens with both:

1. $A \lor (B \lor C)$

   Here the main connective is the $\lor$ on the left. The sentence also involves three letters, which means that in writing out the possible combination we are going to take a little more space. Looking at the sentence is enough to suggest it could be false, whatever A, B, and C mean. Here is the procedure for determining whether this one is a tautology:

A	$\lor$	(B	$\lor$	C)
T		T		T
T		T		F
T		F		T
T		F		F
F		T		T
F		T		F
F		F		T
F		F		F

Now to do the disjunction inside the most brackets:

A	∨	(B	∨	C)
T		T	**T**	T
T		T	**T**	F
T		F	**T**	T
T		F	**F**	F
F		T	**T**	T
F		T	**T**	F
F		F	**T**	T
F		F	**F**	F

Now the remaining column:

A	∨	(B	∨	C)
T	**T**	T	T	T
T	**T**	T	T	F
T	**T**	F	T	T
T	**T**	F	F	F
F	**T**	T	T	T
F	**T**	T	T	F
F	**T**	F	T	T
F	**F**	F	F	F

We see that there is one line in which this sentence is false, so it is not a tautology. Let us see what happens if we take the other reading of $A \lor B \lor C$:

2. $(A \lor B) \lor C$

Here the main connective is the ∨ on the right.

(A	∨	B)	∨	C
T		T		T
T		T		F
T		F		T
T		F		F
F		T		T
F		T		F
F		F		T
F		F		F

Now do the disjunction inside the most brackets:

(A	∨	B)	∨	C
T	**T**	T		T
T	**T**	T		F
T	**T**	F		T
T	**T**	F		F
F	**T**	T		T
F	**T**	T		F
F	**F**	F		T
F	**F**	F		F

Now the remaining column:

(A	∨	B)	∨	C
T	T	T	**T**	T
T	T	T	**T**	F
T	T	F	**T**	T
T	T	F	**T**	F
F	T	T	**T**	T
F	T	T	**T**	F
F	F	F	**T**	T
F	F	F	**F**	F

The column under the main connective for both ways of writing the sentence are the same. The two ways are logically equivalent.

[	(A	∨	B)	∨	C	]	≡	[	A	∨	(B	∨	C)	]
	T	T	T	T	T		**T**		T	T	T	T	T	
	T	T	T	T	F		**T**		T	T	T	T	F	
	T	T	F	T	T		**T**		T	T	F	T	T	
	T	T	F	T	F		**T**		T	T	F	F	F	
	F	T	T	T	T		**T**		F	T	T	T	T	
	F	T	T	T	F		**T**		F	T	T	T	F	
	F	F	F	T	T		**T**		F	T	F	T	T	
	F	F	F	F	F		**T**		F	F	F	F	F	

Since $(A \lor B) \lor C$ and $A \lor (B \lor C)$ are true in the same cases, we can put a material equivalence sign between them and generate a tautology.[4] This important result is called the *associative law of disjunction*. Conjunction ($\cdot$) is also associative; it does not matter where you put the brackets. Here is the truth table that shows this:

---

[4] This is not merely a true material equivalence but a tautologous one.

[	A	·	(B	·	C)	]	≡	[	(A	·	B)	·	C	]
	T	T	T	T	T		**T**		T	T	T	T	T	
	T	F	T	F	F		**T**		T	T	T	F	F	
	T	F	F	F	T		**T**		T	F	F	F	T	
	T	F	F	F	F		**T**		T	F	F	F	F	
	F	F	T	T	T		**T**		F	F	T	F	T	
	F	F	T	F	F		**T**		F	F	T	F	F	
	F	F	F	F	T		**T**		F	F	F	F	T	
	F	F	F	F	F		**T**		F	F	F	F	F	

Let us have a look at some more sentences. The variously shaped brackets are to make the sentences easier to see, but there is no difference here between a curved, square, or curly brackets.

$$[\,A \cdot (B \lor C)\,] \equiv [\,(A \cdot B) \lor (A \cdot C)\,]$$

Read this sentence out loud, and you will see that it is fairly simple and intuitively true. "A, and either B or C" has the same truth value as "A and B, or A and C" (remember that "or" is inclusive). Let us see if it is in fact a tautology.

[	A	·	(B	∨	C)	]	≡	[	(A	·	B)	∨	(A	·	C)	]
	T		T		T				T		T		T		T	
	T		T		F				T		T		T		F	
	T		F		T				T		F		T		T	
	T		F		F				T		F		T		F	
	F		T		T				F		T		F		T	
	F		T		F				F		T		F		F	
	F		F		T				F		F		F		T	
	F		F		F				F		F		F		F	

[	A	·	(B	∨	C)	]	≡	[	(A	·	B)	∨	(A	·	C)	]
	T		T	**T**	T				T	**T**	T		T	**T**	T	
	T		T	**T**	F				T	**T**	T		T	**F**	F	
	T		F	**T**	T				T	**F**	F		T	**T**	T	
	T		F	**F**	F				T	**F**	F		T	**F**	F	
	F		T	**T**	T				F	**F**	T		F	**F**	T	
	F		T	**T**	F				F	**F**	T		F	**F**	F	
	F		F	**T**	T				F	**F**	F		F	**F**	T	
	F		F	**F**	F				F	**F**	F		F	**F**	F	

[	A	·	(B	∨	C)	]	≡	[	(A	·	B)	∨	(A	·	C)	]
	T	T	T	T	T				T	T	T	T	T	T	T	
	T	T	T	T	F				T	T	T	T	T	F	F	
	T	T	F	T	T				T	F	F	T	T	T	T	
	T	F	F	F	F				T	F	F	F	T	F	F	
	F	F	T	T	T				F	F	T	F	F	F	T	
	F	F	T	T	F				F	F	T	F	F	F	F	
	F	F	F	T	T				F	F	F	F	F	F	T	
	F	F	F	F	F				F	F	F	F	F	F	F	

[	A	·	(B	∨	C)	]	≡	[	(A	·	B)	∨	(A	·	C)	]
	T	T	T	T	T		**T**		T	T	T	T	T	T	T	
	T	T	T	T	F		**T**		T	T	T	T	T	F	F	
	T	T	F	T	T		**T**		T	F	F	T	T	T	T	
	T	F	F	F	F		**T**		T	F	F	F	T	F	F	
	F	F	T	T	T		**T**		F	F	T	F	F	F	T	
	F	F	T	T	F		**T**		F	F	T	F	F	F	F	
	F	F	F	T	T		**T**		F	F	F	F	F	F	T	
	F	F	F	F	F		**T**		F	F	F	F	F	F	F	

It is a tautology. The sentence that we have shown to be a tautology shows the *distributive law for conjunction*. Let us see if disjunction (∨) is distributive as well.

[	A	∨	(B	·	C)	]	≡	[	(A	∨	B)	·	(A	∨	C)	]
	T	T	T	T	T		**T**		T	T	T	T	T	T	T	
	T	T	T	F	F		**T**		T	T	T	T	T	T	F	
	T	T	F	F	T		**T**		T	F	T	T	T	T	T	
	T	T	F	F	F		**T**		T	F	T	T	T	T	F	
	F	T	T	T	T		**T**		F	F	T	T	F	T	T	
	F	F	T	F	F		**T**		F	F	T	F	F	F	F	
	F	F	F	F	T		**T**		F	F	F	F	F	T	T	
	F	F	F	F	F		**T**		F	F	F	F	F	F	F	

If you are not sure about this truth table then try working it through for yourself. This truth table shows the *distributive law of disjunction*. Finally, let us show the logical equivalence[5] of two ways of writing the exclusive "or."

4.3   How to write the exclusive "or"

Here is one way of writing the exclusive "or":

---

[5]Remember that if $A \equiv B$ is a tautology, then A and B are logically equivalent, but in general the converse does not hold.

$$(A \vee B) \cdot {\sim}(A \cdot B)$$

This states that either A or B but not both. I claim that there is a much simpler way of writing the exclusive "or". Here it is:

$${\sim}(A \equiv B)$$

We can verify this by seeing if the following sentence is a tautology.

$$[\,(A \vee B) \cdot {\sim}(A \cdot B)\,] \equiv {\sim}(A \equiv B)$$

Since the main connective is a material implication ($\equiv$) if the sentence is a tautology, it *must* be the case that $(A \vee B) \cdot {\sim}(A \cdot B)$ has the same truth value as ${\sim}(A \equiv B)$.

To fill out the truth table for this sentence is laborious and time consuming.

[	(A	∨	B)	·	~	(A	·	B)	]	≡	~	(A	≡	B)
	T		T			T		T				T		T
	T		F			T		F				T		F
	F		T			F		T				F		T
	F		F			F		F				F		F

[	(A	∨	B)	·	~	(A	·	B)	]	≡	~	(A	≡	B)
	T	**T**	T			T	**T**	T				T	**T**	T
	T	**T**	F			T	**F**	F				T	**F**	F
	F	**T**	T			F	**F**	T				F	**F**	T
	F	**F**	F			F	**F**	F				F	**T**	F

[	(A	∨	B)	·	~	(A	·	B)	]	≡	~	(A	≡	B)
	T	T	T		**F**	T	T	T			**F**	T	T	T
	T	T	F		**T**	T	F	F			**T**	T	F	F
	F	T	T		**T**	F	F	T			**T**	F	F	T
	F	F	F		**T**	F	F	F			**F**	F	T	F

[	(A	∨	B)	·	~	(A	·	B)	]	≡	~	(A	≡	B)
	T	T	T	**F**	F	T	T	T			F	T	T	T
	T	T	F	**T**	T	T	F	F			T	T	F	F
	F	T	T	**T**	T	F	F	T			T	F	F	T
	F	F	F	**F**	T	F	F	F			F	F	T	F

[	(A	∨	B)	·	~	(A	·	B)	]	≡	~	(A	≡	B)
	T	T	T	F	F	T	T	T		**T**	F	T	T	T
	T	T	F	T	T	T	F	F		**T**	T	T	F	F
	F	T	T	T	T	F	F	T		**T**	T	F	F	T
	F	F	F	F	T	F	F	F		**T**	F	F	T	F

We have just shown that if we want to specify the exclusive "or" we can do it quite simply by saying "A does not have the same truth value as B" as opposed to "A or B but not both." In terms of length $\sim(A \equiv B)$ is the more user-friendly way of writing the exclusive "or'.

Definition 4.3.1 *We introduce a notation convention here. Instead of writing* $\sim(A \equiv B)$ *we may write* $A \not\equiv B$.

4.4   Exercises

Write out the truth table for $A \not\equiv B$.

Use truth-tables to determine whether the following are tautologies.

1. $\sim\sim\sim\sim A \equiv A$

2. $(A \equiv \sim A) \equiv \sim A$

3. $\sim(A \cdot \sim B) \equiv (\sim A \lor B)$

4. $[A \cdot (B \lor C)] \equiv [(A \cdot B) \lor (A \cdot C)]$

5. $[A \lor (B \cdot \sim C)] \equiv \sim[A \cdot (B \cdot C)]$

6. $\sim[A \cdot B] \lor [B \cdot A]$

7. $[A \lor (B \equiv C)] \equiv [(A \lor B) \equiv (A \lor C)]$

8. $[A \cdot (B \equiv \sim C)] \equiv [(A \equiv B) \lor (A \equiv \sim C)]$

9. $(A \not\equiv B) \equiv (A \equiv \sim B)$

10. $\sim[(A \cdot B) \lor C] \lor [\sim(A \cdot \sim C) \cdot (\sim A \lor B)]$

Chapter 5

Material Implication and Validity

The truth tables are purely a mechanical operation on the possible truth values of the embedded sentences. From doing the truth tables, it is easy to see that there are no elements of causality, time, or probability in the truth table method. We will now discuss the conditional ("if... then...") and a truth table analysis of it called *material implication*. In particular we will discuss how a truth table analysis with no causal, temporal or probabilistic import can analyze a connective that is apparently loaded with such implications.

5.1 Material implication in theory

5.1.1 The truth conditions of material implication

At the end of Chapter 2 we very briefly discussed a very troublesome connective, the "if... then..." connective, sometimes called the *conditional*. The problem with it is that in natural language there are all sorts of causal links and strange relevances implied by its use. Moreover, these causal links are not truth functional ("... caused..." is by no means a truth function). However a logic that is to be used to analyze natural language will be almost completely useless if it cannot deal with these problems.

Suppose you walk past a shop and you see a sign saying "If you pay cash then you get 25 per cent off." You then go into the shop and buy something. There are four possible situations:

1. You pay cash and you get 25 per cent off.

2. You pay cash and do not get 25 per cent off.

3. You do not pay cash, you write a cheque, and get 25 per cent off anyway.

4. You do not pay cash, and you do not get 25 per cent off.

In which of these four situations is it obvious that the sign in the shop window was false?

- You can hardly accuse the shopkeeper of a falsehood if you walk in, pay cash and get the 25 per cent off. As a matter of fact it would be considered unusual to say the sign was not anything other than true in this situation.

- Situations 3 and 4 are less clear. Certainly in situation 3 you cannot say that the sign was untrue because you got 25 per cent regardless of whether cash was paid. Indeed, in this case maybe the sign should be said to be true, if a little useless.

- However in situation 2 you do have every right to say the sign is false. If, having seen the sign, someone pays cash and does not get 25 per cent off then he could legitimately say the sign was false, a lie.

What we can say for sure is that in situation 2 the sign is definitely false. What is more, in situation 1 the sign seems to be true; and in the other two situations we do not really know, but we cannot say that it is false, we need more information. Unfortunately, in Propositional Logic there is no truth value "do not know," so we have to give truth values to the sign in situations 3 and 4. It does seem completely mad to say that the sign is false in situations 3 and 4 so there is only one truth value left, so we must say that it is true. This gives us the basis for our analysis of "if...then..." in our logic system. First of all we will have to give it a symbol as it is a truth function:

Definition 5.1.1

Truth Function	Symbols
Material implication (If...then...)	$\supset \Rightarrow \rightarrow$

The symbol we shall use here is the hook $\supset$; it is rarely used to mean anything other than the truth function with the truth table truth table of Def 5.1.3.

Definition 5.1.2 *In any statement involving material implication (of the form $A \supset B$) the first sentence is called the* antecedent *and the second is called the* consequent. *In a sentence like $A \supset B$ the antecedent is A and the consequent is B.*

5.1.2   The truth table for material implication

Remember our truth conditions for "If you pay cash then you will get 25 per cent off"?[1] If the antecedent is true and the consequent is false (the antecedent in our example was "you pay cash" and the consequent was "you get 25 per cent off"), then the sentence is false, otherwise we have no choice but to say that it is true. The truth table for this follows automatically. In this truth table the A refers to the antecedent and the B refers to the consequent.

---

[1]The term "material implication" refers to the truth function given by the truth table below. It refers to the "if...then..." given by truth table analysis. We will mostly ignore the argument about material implication being identical with the conditional of English.

⊃	A	B
T	T	T
F	T	F
T	F	T
T	F	F

Definition 5.1.3

Here we can see that $A \supset B$ is false only when the antecedent A is true and the consequent B is false, otherwise it is true. This is the "if... then..." of mathematics and electronic circuits.

Note also that, like material equivalence, material implication is true purely as a result of the way things happen to be. Hook is true either when the antecedent happens to be false or the consequent happens to be true. However *entailment* or maybe "... implies..." means that there is no way that the antecedent is true while the consequent is false (validity and entailment are extremely similar notions. It would not be unreasonable to define validity as the premises entailing the conclusion), so if $A \supset B$ is a tautology then A entails B, but in general the converse does not hold.

5.1.3 Counterfactuals, a problem for the truth tables

There are counter-examples to this analysis of "if... then..." called *counterfactuals* (a rather outdated term for them is also *subjunctive conditionals* because they use the subjunctive tense). Counterfactuals are conditional sentences like this:

1. If I had jumped out of that window I would have fallen straight down.

2. If Bruce Lee had not died he would have made more films.

On examination of these sentences we see that the antecedents are false, they are contrary-to-the-facts (hence counterfactual).[2] Under the analysis of conditionals we have given (the truth table), if the antecedent is false then the whole thing is true. It is certainly true that the antecedents of both sentences are false. Take sentence (2) for example: Bruce Lee did die. However it seems crazy to say that it is true that if he had stayed alive he would have made more films just because in real life he died. One would say Bruce Lee would have made more films because he was in the process of making one when he died, he enjoyed making them and was becoming a huge success.

With counterfactuals even though the antecedent is false the entire thing can be false as well (suppose that before he died Bruce Lee had decided to pack it in). This is a major blow to our logic, it seems that our analysis of the conditional does not fit.

Clearly a different analysis of the conditional is required for counterfactuals, and countless books have been written on this subject.

---

[2] Strictly speaking, the term "counterfactual" is misleading as such conditionals need not have false antecedents

Spotting counterfactuals

A good way to spot a counterfactual is by the appearance of the word "would" in the consequent. Note that not all counterfactuals use the past tense, for example "I would not do that if I were you." There is no foolproof system for spotting counterfactuals but most seem to involve the past or situations that may be or have been. The word "would" usually indicates a counterfactual conditional. Here are some examples of counterfactuals as distinct from indicative (present tense) counterparts:

1. If there is an elephant in front of me then there is something wrong with my eyes.

2. If there were an elephant in front of me there would be something wrong with my eyes.

Sentence (1) is obviously true, as is the sentence "If there is an elephant in front of me there is nothing wrong with my eyes" (the elephant may be invisible for example). It seems that sentence (1) conforms to the logic (the truth table). The second sentence is obviously false: what has an elephant in front of me got to do with my eyes working properly? Here is another pair:

1. If Ed Wood did not make *Plan 9 from Outer Space* somebody else did.

2. If Ed Wood had not made *Plan 9 from Outer Space* somebody else would have.

Sentence (1) is true, once again the logic fits for this sort of sentence (sometimes called *indicative* conditionals). Consider the truth of the sentence "If Ed Wood did not make *Plan 9 from Outer Space* then nobody did," here both the antecedent and the consequent are false and the whole sentence is still true.[3] However sentence (2) is false – only Ed Wood could have produced *Plan 9 from Outer Space*.

What's up with counterfactuals

The underlying factor in counterfactuals that makes them so different is that they strongly imply a causal link between the antecedent and a consequent. "A caused B" is clearly not truth functional, so counterfactuals are not truth functional. As a matter of fact causation is so strongly mixed up in counterfactuals that many philosophers used counterfactuals to give definitions of causation; e.g. if A caused B then it is true that if A had not happened B would not have happened. There is also a temporal element to counterfactuals, since in many the antecedent refers to the past or the consequent to the future.

---

[3]There is argument here. It would seem that by seeing the film we know that *somebody* made it. However imagine the sentence being said in a similar way the sentence, "If that sandwich is fresh then I am the king of France." If the sandwich is not fresh is it true that if it is, I am the king of France? Opinions differ. For the purposes of this book however the answer is in effect "yes."

Whatever you make of counterfactuals it must be agreed that they should not be translated into propositional logic, and in this book we shall hope (or make sure) they never turn up. What might be true is that our analysis of "if...then..." works for these indicative conditionals; if the antecedent is false it does seem that the whole thing is true no matter what truth value the consequent takes. Again, in the spirit of equally weighted argument, there are many who will not even say that much.

More ignorance

Counterfactuals are not the only problem. Conditionals about the future such as

If I go to the park I will be mugged

seem to evade the truth functional analysis. Not going to the park does not guarantee the truth of the conditional. Also problematic are conditionals over incomplete knowledge such as

If the butler did it then the maid helped him.

But note in these examples that there is a strong temporal and causal element to them.

We shall use the truth tables for the conditional in spite of the problems. Please avoid and ignore conditionals that appear to dislike the truth table analysis, which is very useful aside from the flaws discussed here. It *is* the "if...then..." of much of mathematics and it is frequently used as a component of a more complicated analysis for all conditionals. For example we may say that "if A then B" states the necessity of $A \supset B$ (for some appropriately subtle sense of "necessary").

5.1.4 Material implication does not imply any causality

The analysis of "if...then..." that is suggested by material implication is a truth functional one. That is to say, $A \supset B$ is true or false only because of the *truth values* of A and B. The sentence $A \supset B$ does not imply that there is any causal link between A and B or anything like that. All that $A \supset B$ states is that it happens not to be the case that both A is true and B is false.

The question is: can this analysis be applied to natural language? *Despite its problems material implication* does *display many of the properties of the natural language conditional.* We will assume the answer is "yes." Material implication is an excellent starting point for a logic of validity (amoung other things).

5.1.5 Only if...

There is another type of conditional that is truth functional, the conditional "...only if ...." "A only if B" means it will only be true that A if it is true that B. This means that if it is true that A it is true that B (because A is only true if it is also true that B). So we can read "A only if B" as "if A then B."

Suppose you walk up to a night-club and the bouncer stops you at the door and says "you can come in only if you have a ticket." This means that if you are to get in you must have a ticket. It does not follow that if you have a ticket you can get in; suppose you do have a ticket but the bouncer still will not let you in because you do not have ID. "If A then B" is formalized as $A \supset B$. But if we add an "only" before the "if" to get "Only if A, B" the hook flips around, to get $A \subset B$ or $B \supset A$.

$A \supset B$ = If A then B = A only if B = only if B, A = B, if A.

$B \supset A$ = B only if A = If B then A = only if A, B = A, if B.[4]

Here is another example. A theologian friend of mine is trying to reconcile free will with the following claim:

(∗) God says something only if it is true.

Given (∗) it is easy to see that:

(∗∗) If God says something then it is true.

It should also be easy to see that from (∗∗) we may deduce (∗) (and vise versa). It should be plain that the two sentences are logically equivalent. We can formalize (∗∗) easily into $A \supset B$ for the appropriate A and B. Since (∗) is logically equivalent to (∗∗) then it must also formalize as $A \supset B$. It is hard to comprehend but $A \supset B$ may be read as "A only if B."

Sometimes you will hear expressions like A is *sufficient* for B or that B is *necessary* for A. What people might mean by these expressions is the following: when $A \supset B$ is a tautology (or necessary in some way) then A is sufficient for B, and B is necessary for A. If $A \equiv B$ is a tautology then A is *necessary and sufficient* for B. However the use of "necessary" and "sufficient" is varied, so do not take the above as law.

Many people think that "A only if B" is logically equivalent to "A if and only if B". It is important to remember, however, that $B \supset A$ (A only if B) is not equivalent to $A \equiv B$.

5.2 Material implication in practice

Let us have a look at some sentences involving material implication:

$$(A \equiv B) \equiv [(A \supset B) \cdot (B \supset A)]$$

This sentence says that A and B are materially equivalent when A materially implies B and B materially implies A. This sounds very much as if it should be a tautology.

---

[4]Please excuse the abuse of the identity symbol.

```
(A  ≡  B)  ≡  [  (A  ⊃  B)  ·  (B  ⊃  A)  ]
 T     T         T      T       T      T
 T     F         T      F       T      F
 F     T         F      T       F      T
 F     F         F      F       F      F
```

```
(A  ≡  B)  ≡  [  (A  ⊃  B)  ·  (B  ⊃  A)  ]
 T  T  T         T  T  T       T  T  T
 T  F  F         T  F  F       F  T  T
 F  F  T         F  T  T       T  F  F
 F  T  F         F  T  F       F  T  F
```

```
(A  ≡  B)  ≡  [  (A  ⊃  B)  ·  (B  ⊃  A)  ]
 T  T  T         T  T  T  T  T  T  T
 T  F  F         T  F  F  F  F  T  T
 F  F  T         F  T  T  F  T  F  F
 F  T  F         F  T  F  T  F  T  F
```

```
(A  ≡  B)  ≡  [  (A  ⊃  B)  ·  (B  ⊃  A)  ]
 T  T  T  T      T  T  T  T  T  T  T
 T  F  F  T      T  F  F  F  F  T  T
 F  F  T  T      F  T  T  F  T  F  F
 F  T  F  T      F  T  F  T  F  T  F
```

We can now see an obvious relation between material equivalence and material implication. $A \equiv B$ will always take the same truth values as $A \supset B \cdot B \supset A$. So if A is materially equivalent to B then A materially implies B and B materially implies A.

Here is another sentence:

$$[\,(A \supset B) \cdot (B \supset C)\,] \supset (A \supset C)$$

This sentence says that if A materially implies B and B materially implies C, then A materially implies B. This is quite intuitive.

```
[  (A  ⊃  B)  ·  (B  ⊃  C)  ]  ⊃  (A  ⊃  C)
    T     T   T     T            T     T
    T     T   T     F            T     F
    T     F   F     T            T     T
    T     F   F     F            T     F
    F     T   T     T            F     T
    F     T   T     F            F     F
    F     F   F     T            F     T
    F     F   F     F            F     F
```

[(A	⊃	B)	·	(B	⊃	C)	] ⊃	(A	⊃	C)
T	**T**	T		T	**T**	T		T	**T**	T
T	**T**	T		T	**F**	F		T	**F**	F
T	**F**	F		F	**T**	T		T	**T**	T
T	**F**	F		F	**T**	F		T	**F**	F
F	**T**	T		T	**T**	T		F	**T**	T
F	**T**	T		T	**F**	F		F	**T**	F
F	**T**	F		F	**T**	T		F	**T**	T
F	**T**	F		F	**T**	F		F	**T**	F

[(A	⊃	B)	·	(B	⊃	C)	] ⊃	(A	⊃	C)
T	T	T	**T**	T	T	T		T	T	T
T	T	T	**F**	T	F	F		T	F	F
T	F	F	**F**	F	T	T		T	T	T
T	F	F	**F**	F	T	F		T	F	F
F	T	T	**T**	T	T	T		F	T	T
F	T	T	**F**	T	F	F		F	T	F
F	T	F	**T**	F	T	T		F	T	T
F	T	F	**T**	F	T	F		F	T	F

[(A	⊃	B)	·	(B	⊃	C)	] ⊃	(A	⊃	C)
T	T	T	T	T	T	T	**T**	T	T	T
T	T	T	F	T	F	F	**T**	T	F	F
T	F	F	F	F	T	T	**T**	T	T	T
T	F	F	F	F	T	F	**T**	T	F	F
F	T	T	T	T	T	T	**T**	F	T	T
F	T	T	F	T	F	F	**T**	F	T	F
F	T	F	T	F	T	T	**T**	F	T	T
F	T	F	T	F	T	F	**T**	F	T	F

This tautology shows the *transitivity of material implication*. A relation between two objects is transitive when if *x* relates to *y* and *y* relates to *z*, then *x* relates to *z*. Examples of transitive relations are "... is to the right of..." or "... is an ancestor of..." and as we have shown here, "... materially implies...."

Now we have all that is necessary to deal with any truth functional sentence of natural language. We can translate it into propositional logic and then determine whether it is a tautology or not. As a matter of fact we have now done enough to be able to prove all the tautologies of propositional logic. However all the tautologies of propositional logic are not all the necessary truths of natural language.[5] However, this does not mean that when using propositional logic we

---

[5] "All bachelors are unmarried" is an example of a necessary truth that does not show up in propositional logic as it can only be formalized using a single letter: e.g. *A* (where *A* is "All bachelors are unmarried"). When we form a truth table for a sentence that is merely a single letter we will find that it is not a tautology. Here is as far as you can go with the truth

will churn out incorrect results.[6]

$$\sim \sim A \equiv A$$

This sentence may be read: it is false that A is false has the same truth value as A.

$$
\begin{array}{ccccc}
\sim & \sim & A & \equiv & A \\
 & & T & & T \\
 & & F & & F
\end{array}
$$

$$
\begin{array}{ccccc}
\sim & \sim & A & \equiv & A \\
 & F & T & & T \\
 & T & F & & F
\end{array}
$$

$$
\begin{array}{ccccc}
\sim & \sim & A & \equiv & A \\
T & F & T & & T \\
F & T & F & & F
\end{array}
$$

$$
\begin{array}{ccccc}
\sim & \sim & A & \equiv & A \\
T & F & T & T & T \\
F & T & F & T & F
\end{array}
$$

This is the famous rule of double negation which some logic systems deny. Of course in order to do this they have to say that truth tables should not be used.

5.2.1 More interesting tautologies

Remember that in this logic the laws of non-contradiction and excluded middle are logically equivalent? Here is a similar result on the relation between $\vee$ and $\supset$.

$$(A \vee B) \equiv (\sim A \supset B)$$

The truth table:

$$
\begin{array}{ccccccc}
(A & \vee & B) & \equiv & (\sim & A & \supset & B) \\
T & T & & & & T & & T \\
T & F & & & & T & & F \\
F & T & & & & F & & T \\
F & F & & & & F & & F
\end{array}
$$

table:

$$
\begin{array}{c}
A \\
T \\
F
\end{array}
$$

This is definitely not a tautology (a tautology must finish its truth table with a column of Ts).

[6]The notion of validity and tautology are not a part of propositional logic logic but are meta-notions. Propositional logic itself says nothing about validity and tautologies; it is only in us *looking* at the logic that the terms "valid" and "tautology" have meaning.

(A	V	B)	≡	(~	A	⊃	B)
T	**T**	T		**F**	T		T
T	**T**	F		**F**	T		F
F	**T**	T		**T**	F		T
F	**F**	F		**T**	F		F

(A	V	B)	≡	(~	A	⊃	B)
T	**T**	T		F	T	**T**	T
T	**T**	F		F	T	**T**	F
F	**T**	T		T	F	**T**	T
F	**F**	F		T	F	**F**	F

(A	V	B)	≡	(~	A	⊃	B)
T	T	T	**T**	F	T	T	T
T	T	F	**T**	F	T	T	F
F	T	T	**T**	T	F	T	T
F	F	F	**T**	·T	F	F	F

A tautology. Check that the following are tautologies for yourself (where mt. equ. means materially equivalent):

1. $(A \lor B) \equiv (\sim A \supset B)$ "A or B" is mt. equ. to "If not A then B"

2. $(A \lor B) \equiv (\sim B \supset A)$ "A or B" is mt. equ. to "If not B then A"

3. $(A \lor B) \equiv [\,(\sim A \supset B) \cdot (\sim B \supset A)\,]$

It should be clear that the following is a tautology:

$$(A \lor \sim A) \equiv (\sim \sim A \supset A)$$

Here is the truth table for the benefit of the cynics:

(A	V	~	A)	⊃	(~	~	A	⊃	A)
T	T	F	T	**T**	T	F	T	T	T
F	T	T	F	**T**	F	T	F	T	F

Here is another sentence:

$$\sim(A \cdot B) \equiv (A \supset \sim B)$$

Here is how to do the truth table:

~	(A	·	B)	≡	(A	⊃	~	B)
	T		T		T			T
	T		F		T			F
	F		T		F			T
	F		F		F			F

~	(A	·	B)	≡	(A	⊃	~	B)
	T	**T**	T		T		**F**	T
	T	**F**	F		T		**T**	F
	F	**F**	T		F		**F**	T
	F	**F**	F		F		**T**	F

~	(A	·	B)	≡	(A	⊃	~	B)
F	T	T	T		T	**F**	F	T
T	T	F	F		T	**T**	T	F
T	F	F	T		F	**T**	F	T
T	F	F	F		F	**T**	T	F

~	(A	·	B)	≡	(A	⊃	~	B)
F	T	T	T	**T**	T	F	F	T
T	T	F	F	**T**	T	T	T	F
T	F	F	T	**T**	F	T	F	T
T	F	F	F	**T**	F	T	T	F

It should be easy to see that the following are also tautologies, check them for yourself:

1. $\sim(A \cdot B) \equiv (A \supset \sim B)$

2. $\sim(A \cdot B) \equiv (B \supset \sim A)$

3. $\sim(A \cdot B) \equiv [\,(B \supset \sim A) \cdot (B \supset \sim A)\,]$

Here is another tautology that it is very helpful to know.

$$(A \supset B) \equiv (\sim B \supset \sim A)$$

According to this sentence if A materially implies B then if B is not true, A is not true. It should be obvious with a little thought that the sentence is a tautology. Of course what comes next is a tedious truth table:

(A	⊃	B)	≡	(~	B	⊃	~	A)
T		T			T			T
T		F			F			T
F		T			T			F
F		F			F			F

(A	⊃	B)	≡	(~	B	⊃	~	A)
T	**T**	T		**F**	T		**F**	T
T	**F**	F		**T**	F		**F**	T
F	**T**	T		**F**	T		**T**	F
F	**T**	F		**T**	F		**T**	F

$(A$	$\supset$	$B)$	$\equiv$	$(\sim$	B	$\supset$	$\sim$	$A)$
T	T	T		F	T	T	F	T
T	F	F		T	F	F	F	T
F	T	T		F	T	T	T	F
F	T	F		T	F	T	T	F

$(A$	$\supset$	$B)$	$\equiv$	$(\sim$	B	$\supset$	$\sim$	$A)$
T	T	T	$\mathbf{T}$	F	T	T	F	T
T	F	F	$\mathbf{T}$	T	F	F	F	T
F	T	T	$\mathbf{T}$	F	T	T	T	F
F	T	F	$\mathbf{T}$	T	F	T	T	F

This is the law of *contra-position*.

5.2.2 DeMorgan's Laws

These laws are very important and it is useful to remember them (though not imperative).[7]

$$(\sim A \vee \sim B) \equiv \sim (A \cdot B)$$

The above is a be a tautology. The sentence "Either A is not true or B is not true" is logically equivalent[8] to the sentence "A and B are not both true."

$(\sim$	A	$\vee$	$\sim$	$B)$	$\equiv$	$\sim$	$(A$	$\cdot$	$B)$
F	T	F	F	T	$\mathbf{T}$	F	T	T	T
F	T	T	T	F	$\mathbf{T}$	T	T	F	F
T	F	T	F	T	$\mathbf{T}$	T	F	F	T
T	F	T	T	F	$\mathbf{T}$	T	F	F	F

Here is the other law.

$$(\sim A \cdot \sim B) \equiv \sim (A \vee B)$$

The sentence "It is not the case that A and it is also not the case that B" is logically equivalent to "neither A nor B." So the above should be a tautology.

$(\sim$	A	$\cdot$	$\sim$	$B)$	$\equiv$	$\sim$	$(A$	$\vee$	$B)$
F	T	F	F	T	$\mathbf{T}$	F	T	T	T
F	T	F	T	F	$\mathbf{T}$	F	T	T	F
T	F	F	F	T	$\mathbf{T}$	F	F	T	T
T	F	T	T	F	$\mathbf{T}$	T	F	F	F

These two laws are called *DeMorgan's laws*.

---

[7]DeMorgan's and the laws above are of significance (to be called laws) in other contexts and logic systems. Their importance lies in fundamental disputes about the nature of certain logical relations and systems.

[8]Note that the beginnings of a promising analysis of logical equivalence between A and B, is that $A \equiv B$ is tautology.

1. $\sim(A \cdot B) \equiv (\sim A \vee \sim B)$

2. $\sim(A \vee B) \equiv (\sim A \cdot \sim B)$

We can write two more sentences which are very similar. It should be easy to see that they are tautologies.

1. $(A \cdot B) \equiv \sim(\sim A \vee \sim B)$

2. $(A \vee B) \equiv \sim(\sim A \cdot \sim B)$

Can you see how all these sentences are tautologies? All we have done is to move the negation from one side of the $\equiv$ to the other. This suggests that this should be a tautology:

(A	$\equiv$	$\sim$	B)	$\equiv$	($\sim$	A	$\equiv$	B)
T	F	F	T	**T**	F	T	F	T
T	T	T	F	**T**	F	T	T	F
F	T	F	T	**T**	T	F	T	T
F	F	T	F	**T**	T	F	F	F

So we can see that it does not matter which side of the material equivalence symbol the negation is on; $A \equiv \sim B$ is logically equivalent to $\sim A \equiv B$. Here is another rather useful law for how material implication can be rewritten:

(A	$\supset$	B)	$\equiv$	$\sim$	(A	$\cdot$	$\sim$	B)
T	T	F	**T**	T	T	F	F	T
T	F	T	**T**	F	T	T	T	F
F	T	F	**T**	T	T	F	F	T
F	T	T	**T**	T	T	F	T	F

Since $(A \supset B) \equiv \sim(A \cdot B)$ is a tautology we may say that "If A then B" always has the same truth value as "it is not the case that (both) A and not B."

5.2.3 Some jolly big truth tables

Here are some jolly big truth tables:

$$[(A \equiv B) \cdot (A \equiv C)] \supset (B \equiv C)$$

This is going to be long and boring:

[(A	$\equiv$	B)	$\cdot$	(A	$\equiv$	C)	]	$\supset$	(B	$\equiv$	C)
T	T	T		T	T	T			T	T	T
T	T	T		T	F	F			T	F	F
T	F	F		T	T	T			F	F	T
T	F	F		T	F	F			F	F	F
F	T	T		F	F	T			T	T	T
F	T	T		F	F	F			T	T	F
F	F	F		F	T	T			F	F	T
F	F	F		F	F	F			F	F	F

[	(A	≡	B)	·	(A	≡	C)	]	⊃	(B	≡	C)
	T	**T**	T		T	**T**	T			T	**T**	T
	T	**T**	T		T	**F**	F			T	**F**	F
	T	**F**	F		T	**T**	T			F	**F**	T
	T	**F**	F		T	**F**	F			F	**T**	F
	F	**F**	T		F	**F**	T			T	**T**	T
	F	**F**	T		F	**T**	F			T	**F**	F
	F	**T**	F		F	**F**	T			F	**F**	T
	F	**T**	F		F	**T**	F			F	**T**	F

[	(A	≡	B)	·	(A	≡	C)	]	⊃	(B	≡	C)
	T	T	T	**T**	T	T	T			T	T	T
	T	T	T	**F**	T	F	F			T	F	F
	T	F	F	**F**	T	T	T			F	F	T
	T	F	F	**F**	T	F	F			F	T	F
	F	F	T	**F**	F	F	T			T	T	T
	F	F	T	**F**	F	T	F			T	F	F
	F	T	F	**F**	F	F	T			F	F	T
	F	T	F	**T**	F	T	F			F	T	F

[	(A	≡	B)	·	(A	≡	C)	]	⊃	(B	≡	C)
	T	T	T	T	T	T	T	**T**	T	T	T	
	T	T	T	F	T	F	F	**T**	T	F	F	
	T	F	F	F	T	T	T	**T**	F	F	T	
	T	F	F	F	T	F	F	**T**	F	T	F	
	F	F	T	F	F	F	T	**T**	T	T	T	
	F	F	T	F	F	T	F	**T**	T	F	F	
	F	T	F	F	F	F	T	**T**	F	F	T	
	F	T	F	T	F	T	F	**T**	F	T	F	

So the sentence is a tautology. Is this not incredible?

$$(A \supset B) \vee (B \supset A)$$

Let us see if this is a tautology.

(A	⊃	B)	∨	(B	⊃	A)
T		T		T		T
T		F		F		T
F		T		T		F
F		F		F		F

(A	⊃	B)	∨	(B	⊃	A)
T	**T**	T		T	**T**	T
T	**F**	F		F	**T**	T
F	**T**	T		T	**F**	F
F	**T**	F		F	**T**	F

$$
\begin{array}{ccccccc}
(A & \supset & B) & \lor & (B & \supset & A) \\
T & T & T & \mathbf{T} & T & T & T \\
T & F & F & \mathbf{T} & F & T & T \\
F & T & T & \mathbf{T} & T & F & F \\
F & T & F & \mathbf{T} & F & T & F \\
\end{array}
$$

Is this sentence a tautology?

$$A \lor (B \lor (C \lor (D \lor (E \lor (F \lor G)))))$$

It is certainly not. In order to show it is not a tautology we need only show that (at least) one line of the truth table has an F under the main connective. For the above sentence it just so happens that there is only one such line:

$$
\begin{array}{ccccccccccccc}
A & \lor & (B & \lor & (C & \lor & (D & \lor & (E & \lor & (F & \lor & G))))) \\
F & \mathbf{F} & F & F & F & F & F & F & F & F & F & F & F \\
\end{array}
$$

That was easy, but in order to show that the following sentence is a tautology (which it is):

$$A \lor (B \lor (C \lor (D \lor (E \lor (F \lor {\sim}A)))))$$

we would need to write a truth table $2^6 = 64$ rows long. Therefore if all you want to show is that a particular sentence is *not* a tautology you need only write one line of its truth table in which there is an F under the main connective. But in order to show a sentence to *be* a tautology you need to write out the entire truth table. In the next chapters we shall develop a quicker method of determining whether sentences are tautologies or not.

5.3 Truth tables for analysing arguments

We now have all we need to analyze the validity of some arguments. First let us review on what it is for an argument to be valid. Take this argument:

$$
\begin{array}{c}
P_1 \\
P_2 \\
P_3 \\
\vdots \\
\dfrac{P_n}{C}
\end{array}
$$

There are n premises and a conclusion. The argument is valid when it is impossible for the premises to be true and the conclusion be false. In our logic system, the argument above is valid when the following sentence is a *tautology*:

$${\sim}(P_1 \cdot P_2 \cdot P_3 \cdot \ldots P_n \cdot {\sim}C)$$

This sentence says it is not the case that all the Ps are true and C (the conclusion) is false. Because of the associativity of conjunction we can put some brackets wherever we like.

$$\sim((P_1 \cdot P_2 \cdot P_3 \cdot \ldots P_n) \cdot \sim C)$$

We have only recently seen this format of sentence and how it can be rewritten. Remember that $A \supset B$ is logically equivalent to $\sim(A \cdot \sim B)$? Well we can now rewrite the whole sentence using material implication.

$$(P_1 \cdot P_2 \cdot P_3 \cdot \ldots \cdot P_n) \supset C$$

For any argument we can check its validity by writing a sentence in propositional logic and seeing if it is a tautology. The sentence is of the form

conjunction of premises $\supset$ conclusion

if it is a tautology then the argument is valid. This is because if the sentence we produce from the argument is not a tautology then there is a way the premises can be true and the conclusion can be false (the only way a material implication can be false is if the antecedent is true and the consequent is false). Let us try this out on some famous arguments. Take Modus Ponens:

$$\begin{array}{c} A \\ \underline{A \supset B} \\ B \end{array}$$

We can now rewrite this as one sentence in propositional logic:

$$[\, A \cdot (A \supset B) \,] \supset B$$

Now we can do the logic on it. If the sentence is a tautology, then the argument is valid.

[	A	$\cdot$	(A	$\supset$	B)	]	$\supset$	B
	T	T	T	T	T		T	T
	T	F	T	F	F		T	F
	F	F	F	T	T		T	T
	F	F	F	T	F		T	F

The sentence is a tautology. Therefore in propositional logic, Modus Ponens is a valid argument (as a matter of fact in all useful logics Modus Ponens is a valid argument). Let us try this out on some arguments in natural language.

> Peter likes haddock or cod
> If Peter likes cod then he does not like mushy peas
> <u>Peter likes mushy peas</u>
> Peter likes haddock

We can formalize this using three letters:

$$A \lor B$$
$$B \supset \sim C$$
$$\underline{C}$$
$$A$$

Key
A = Peter Likes haddock
B = Peter likes cod
C = Peter like mushy peas

We can now write this as a sentence in propositional logic (keeping in mind the above key).

$$[\,(A \lor B) \cdot (B \supset \sim C) \cdot C\,] \supset A$$

We will have to rewrite this so we do not get two conjunctions in the same bracket. It does not matter which two we bracket off (see footnote, page 58):

$$[\,(A \lor B) \cdot [\,(B \supset \sim C) \cdot C\,]\,] \supset A$$

Now we do the logic on it. It will be a rather large and cumbersome truth table, but if it shows the sentence to be a tautology, we know the argument is valid.

[	(A	∨	B)	·	[	(B	⊃	~	C)	·	C	]	]	⊃	A
	T		T			T			T		T				T
	T		T			T			F		F				T
	T		F			F			T		T				T
	T		F			F			F		F				T
	F		T			T			T		T				F
	F		T			T			F		F				F
	F		F			F			T		T				F
	F		F			F			F		F				F

[	(A	∨	B)	·	[	(B	⊃	~	C)	·	C	]	]	⊃	A
	T	**T**	T			T		**F**	T		T				T
	T	**T**	T			T		**T**	F		F				T
	T	**T**	F			F		**F**	T		T				T
	T	**T**	F			F		**T**	F		F				T
	F	**T**	T			T		**F**	T		T				F
	F	**T**	T			T		**T**	F		F				F
	F	**F**	F			F		**F**	T		T				F
	F	**F**	F			F		**T**	F		F				F

Table 1

[	(A	∨	B)	·	[	(B	⊃	~	C)	·	C	]	]	⊃	A
	T	T	T			T	F	F	T		T				T
	T	T	T			T	T	T	F		F				T
	T	T	F			F	T	F	T		T				T
	T	T	F			F	T	T	F		F				T
	F	T	T			T	F	F	T		T				F
	F	T	T			T	T	T	F		F				F
	F	F	F			F	T	F	T		T				F
	F	F	F			F	T	T	F		F				F

Table 2

[	(A	∨	B)	·	[	(B	⊃	~	C)	·	C	]	]	⊃	A
	T	T	T			T	F	F	T	F	T				T
	T	T	T			T	T	T	F	F	F				T
	T	T	F			F	T	F	T	T	T				T
	T	T	F			F	T	T	F	F	F				T
	F	T	T			T	F	F	T	F	T				F
	F	T	T			T	T	T	F	F	F				F
	F	F	F			F	T	F	T	T	T				F
	F	F	F			F	T	T	F	F	F				F

Table 3

[	(A	∨	B)	·	[	(B	⊃	~	C)	·	C	]	]	⊃	A
	T	T	T	F		T	F	F	T	F	T				T
	T	T	T	F		T	T	T	F	F	F				T
	T	T	F	T		F	T	F	T	T	T				T
	T	T	F	F		F	T	T	F	F	F				T
	F	T	T	F		T	F	F	T	F	T				F
	F	T	T	F		T	T	T	F	F	F				F
	F	F	F	F		F	T	F	T	T	T				F
	F	F	F	F		F	T	T	F	F	F				F

Table 4

[	(A	∨	B)	·	[	(B	⊃	~	C)	·	C	]	]	⊃	A
	T	T	T	F		T	F	F	T	F	T			T	T
	T	T	T	F		T	T	T	F	F	F			T	T
	T	T	F	T		F	T	F	T	T	T			T	T
	T	T	F	F		F	T	T	F	F	F			T	T
	F	T	T	F		T	F	F	T	F	T			T	F
	F	T	T	F		T	T	T	F	F	F			T	F
	F	F	F	F		F	T	F	T	T	T			T	F
	F	F	F	F		F	T	T	F	F	F			T	F

We can see that the sentence is a tautology, therefore the argument is valid.

Let us try another. Here is a famous fallacy that people make constantly without realising it:

If the management is sexist then few employees are women

Few employees are women
_____

The management is sexist

We can formalize this quite easily:

$$A \supset B$$
$$\underline{B}$$
$$A$$

Key
_____

A = The management is sexist

B = Few employees are women

We can write this as a sentence in propositional logic.

$$[(A \supset B) \cdot B] \supset A$$

Now we check to see if it is a tautology.

[	(A	⊃	B)	·	B	]	⊃	A
	T	T	T	T	T		T	T
	T	F	F	F	F		T	T
	F	T	T	T	T		F	F
	F	T	F	F	F		T	F

The sentence is not a tautology, so the argument is not valid. The argument we have just analyzed is called the *fallacy of affirming the consequent* (occasionally called Modus Morons as a joke) and is the classic invalid argument.

As you may have noticed, analysing arguments like takes up a lot of time an space. Just imagine what would happen if the argument involved four or more letters! If our logic is going to be of any use, it is necessary to come up with a deduction system that is quicker and a lot less cumbersome than the truth table method.

5.4 Exercises

Determine whether the following are tautologies using truth tables (or any technique deriving from truth tables).

1. $[A \supset (B \supset C)] \supset [(A \supset B) \supset (A \supset C)]$

2. $(A \supset B) \equiv (\sim B \supset \sim A)$

3. $(A \equiv B) \equiv [(A \supset B) \cdot (B \supset A)]$

4. $[(A \supset B) \cdot (A \supset C)] \supset [A \supset (B \cdot C)]$

5. $[(A \supset B) \cdot (C \supset B)] \supset [(A \vee C) \supset B]$

6. $\sim A \supset (A \supset A)$

7. $A \supset (\sim A \supset B)$

8. $[(A \cdot B) \vee (\sim A \cdot \sim B)] \equiv (A \equiv B)$

9. $[A \supset B) \supset (B \supset C)] \supset (A \supset C)$

10. $(A \supset B) \vee (B \supset A)$

Chapter 6

The Tableaux Method

6.1 Indirect Proof: a preliminary

It has already been stipulated that we need a quicker and less cumbersome method of showing whether sentences in propositional logic are in fact tautologies. The tableau system is a family of systems in which there are many variants. The system we shall develop here (presented in the next section) is not only the simplest of all the tableau systems but, the simplest of all the deductive systems in that it is very easy to see what is going on. Consider the following sentence:

$$(A \supset B) \supset [\, (B \supset C) \supset (A \supset C)\,]$$

If you read this sentence out aloud (translated back into natural language) you will see that it is a tautology. It says "if A materially implies B, then if a B materially implies C, A materially implies C" (see page 70). We will verify that this sentence is a tautology using a method called *indirect proof*.

Definition 6.1.1 *The method of indirect proof is to assume that the sentence in question is false and then to consider all cases in which this might be. If all the cases are contradictory, then there is no way that that sentence can be false, so it is necessarily true.*[1]

Here is how the reasoning might work. We assume that the sentence is false, writing it like this.

$$(A \ \supset \ B) \ \underset{\mathbf{F}}{\supset} \ [\ (B \ \supset \ C) \ \supset \ (A \ \supset \ C)\ ]$$

Now since the main connective is a $\supset$ there is only one way in which it can be false: if the antecedent is true and the consequent is false.

---

[1] This is not to be confused with *reductio ad absurdum* (or "reductio" for short). The method of reductio is to show something is *false* by assuming it is true and deriving a contradiction. It is similar to indirect proof, but some systems deny the acceptability of one while maintaining the other.

83

$$(A \supset B) \supset [(B \supset C) \supset (A \supset C)]$$
$$\quad\quad\text{T}\quad\quad\text{F}\quad\quad\quad\quad\quad\quad\quad\text{F}$$

On the left hand side there is a true material implication, since there are three ways in which this can happen we will put this side on hold. The right hand side is easier as it is a false material implication, which occurs in only one way.

$$(A \supset B) \supset [(B \supset C) \supset (A \supset C)]$$
$$\quad\quad T \quad\quad F \quad\quad\quad \text{T} \quad F \quad\quad \text{F}$$

Again let us follow the false material implications because they are easier:

$$(A \supset B) \supset [(B \supset C) \supset (A \supset C)]$$
$$\quad\quad T \quad\quad F \quad\quad\quad T \quad\quad F\ T\ F\quad F$$

Now we have put some truth values under actual letters. Because of this we must put the same truth values under all the other places where that letter appears in the sentence:

$$(A \supset B) \supset [(B \supset C) \supset (A \supset C)]$$
$$\text{T}\ \ T \quad\quad F \quad\quad\quad T\ \ \text{F}\ \ F\ \ T\ \ F\ \ F$$

Having filled in these new columns we can see that it narrows down the possibilities for in what way the true material implications are going to be true. Let us do the true material implication on the far left, the $A \supset B$. We know that it is true and that the A is true. Looking at the truth table for material implication, we see that a material implication with a true antecedent can be true only if the consequent is also true:

$\supset$	A	B
T	T	T
F	T	F

The rows in which the antecedent is true.

$\supset$	A	B
T	F	T
T	F	F

$\supset$	A	B
T	T	T

The row where the antcedent is true the whole material implication is true.

$\supset$	A	B
F	T	F
T	F	T
T	F	F

So we know that if $A \supset B$ on the far left of the sentence is to be true with A being true as well, then B should be true also. We can write this in.

$$(A \supset B) \supset [(B \supset C) \supset (A \supset C)]$$
$$T\ \ T\ \ \text{T} \quad F \quad\quad\quad T\ \ F\ \ F\ \ T\ \ F\ \ F$$

Since there is another B in the sentence, we must fill that in with the same truth value: T.

$$(A \quad \supset \quad B) \quad \supset \quad [\quad (B \quad \supset \quad C) \quad \supset \quad (A \quad \supset \quad C) \quad]$$
$$T \quad T \quad T \quad F \qquad \textbf{T} \quad T \quad F \quad F \quad T \quad F \quad F$$

There is a contradiction here, look at the following outlined material implication:

$$(A \quad \supset \quad B) \quad \supset \quad [\; \boxed{(B \quad \supset \quad C)} \quad \supset \quad (A \quad \supset \quad C) \quad]$$
$$T \quad T \quad T \quad F \qquad \boxed{T \quad T \quad F} \quad F \quad T \quad F \quad F$$

The material implication is supposed to be true, yet the consequent is false and the antecedent true. If we look in the truth table for $\supset$ we see that this is exactly when '$\supset$ is false (when the antecedent is true and the consequent is false). There are two possibilities for how this could happen; the first is that we have made a mistake. But there are no printing errors anywhere, and there is certainly nothing wrong with my reasoning. Maybe we should not have done things in the order we did, maybe we should have done the other true material implication first. Let us go back and see.

$$(A \quad \supset \quad B) \quad \supset \quad [\quad (B \quad \supset \quad C) \quad \supset \quad (A \quad \supset \quad C) \quad]$$
$$T \quad T \qquad F \qquad T \quad F \quad F \quad T \quad F \quad F$$

When we got to this point before we filled in the $A \supset B$ on the far left, maybe we should have filled in the $B \supset C$ in the middle instead. It is a true material implication with a false consequent. If you look at the truth table for $\supset$, you will see that the only way you get this is with a false antecedent:

$\supset$	**A**	**B**
T	T	T
F	T	F
T	F	T
T	F	F

The only row where the "$\supset$" is true and the consequent is false.

$$(A \quad \supset \quad B) \quad \supset \quad [\quad (B \quad \supset \quad C) \quad \supset \quad (A \quad \supset \quad C) \quad]$$
$$T \quad T \qquad F \qquad \textbf{F} \quad T \quad F \quad F \quad T \quad F \quad F$$

We must now fill in all the other columns under a B.

$$(A \quad \supset \quad B) \quad \supset \quad [\quad (B \quad \supset \quad C) \quad \supset \quad (A \quad \supset \quad C) \quad]$$
$$T \quad T \quad \textbf{F} \quad F \qquad F \quad T \quad F \quad F \quad T \quad F \quad F$$

We have exactly the same contradiction here as well: we have a material implication that is supposed to be true, yet it has a true antecedent and a false consequent.

$$\boxed{(A \quad \supset \quad B)} \quad \supset \quad [\quad (B \quad \supset \quad C) \quad \supset \quad (A \quad \supset \quad C) \quad]$$
$$\boxed{T \quad T \quad F} \quad F \qquad F \quad T \quad F \quad F \quad T \quad F \quad F$$

The only other explanation for this inescapable contradiction is that it is impossible for the entire sentence to be false (we assumed the sentence to be false and then showed that it led to an absurdity or contradiction). If the sentence cannot be false, then it must always true and hence be a tautology.

6.2   The way of the tableau for tautologies

The method of finding tautologies we have just used is not the best of systems for carrying out an indirect proof. We want to produce a way of doing exactly the same thing more easily and quickly. The tableau method is such a system. Let us go back to the original sentence:

$$(A \supset B) \supset [(B \supset C) \supset (A \supset C)]$$

We will now construct a tableau. First we assume that the sentence is false.

$$\textbf{F}\quad (A \supset B) \supset [(B \supset C) \supset (A \supset C)]$$

Because there is only one way a material implication (the main connective) can be false, we know that the $A \supset B$ must be true and the $(B \supset C) \supset (A \supset C)$ must be false. We write this out underneath the first sentence, we also tick the first sentence so we know we have used it.

$$\textbf{F}\quad (A \supset B) \supset [(B \supset C) \supset (A \supset C)]\ \checkmark$$
$$\textbf{T}\quad A \supset B$$
$$\textbf{F}\quad (B \supset C) \supset (A \supset C)$$

As a general rule there is a lot less work involved if we deal with the sentences that have only one way in which they can be true or false (depending on the letter beside them).

There is only one way to deal with the $(B \supset C) \supset (A \supset C)$ as there is only one way it can be false,[2] so we bring down that line next.

$$\textbf{F}\quad (A \supset B) \supset [(B \supset C) \supset (A \supset C)]\ \checkmark$$
$$\textbf{T}\quad A \supset B$$
$$\textbf{F}\quad (B \supset C) \supset (A \supset C)\ \checkmark$$
$$\textbf{T}\quad B \supset C$$
$$\textbf{F}\quad A \supset C$$

Next we will bring down the $(A \supset C)$ as there is only one way that it can be false.[3]

$$\textbf{F}\quad (A \supset B) \supset [(B \supset C) \supset (A \supset C)]\ \checkmark$$
$$\textbf{T}\quad A \supset B$$
$$\textbf{F}\quad (B \supset C) \supset (A \supset C)\ \checkmark$$
$$\textbf{T}\quad B \supset C$$
$$\textbf{F}\quad A \supset C\ \checkmark$$
$$\textbf{T}\quad A$$
$$\textbf{F}\quad C$$

Now we have to bring down one of the true material implications that we have not ticked off. There are three ways a material implication can be true (look at the truth table), but consider this tautology (compare with page 71):

[2]If $(B \supset C)$ is true and $(A \supset C)$ is false.
[3]If A is true and C is false.

$$(A \supset B) \equiv (\sim A \vee B)$$

So $A \supset B$ has the same truth conditions as, "either it is not the case that A or it is true that B." Although there are three ways in which the material implication can be true, we can express a true $\supset$ just by saying that either A is false or B is true (when we say A is false we are dealing with two of the three possibilities). Look at the truth table:

$\supset$	A	B
T	T	T
F	T	F
T	F	T
T	F	F

— Either B is true...

...or A is false

We express these cases in our tableau like this:

F	$(A \supset B) \supset [\,(B \supset C) \supset (A \supset C)\,]$ $\checkmark$
T	$A \supset B$ $\checkmark$
F	$(B \supset C) \supset (A \supset C)$ $\checkmark$
T	$B \supset C$
F	$A \supset C$ $\checkmark$
T	A
F	C

F A T B
×

The reason we write it like this is that we are considering possibilities. There are two ways[4] in which the material implication as true so we do two branches, one for each possibility.

The × signifies a contradiction. If you look above the × you will see the line

    F A

and further up the branch there is a line

    T A

This is a contradiction, for A cannot both be true and false. *Each branch of the tableaux represents a possible case, and if one contains a contradiction we can rule it out as a possibility.*

There is only one sentence that we have not yet ticked, so we must bring it down into both branches as it must figure in both possibilities. However in this case we only need to bring it down to the right branch as the left branch has a contradiction.

---

[4]We can compress the three lines of the truth table into two cases.

$$\begin{array}{ll} \textbf{F} & (A \supset B) \supset [\,(B \supset C) \supset (A \supset C)\,]\ \checkmark \\ \textbf{T} & A \supset B\ \checkmark \\ \textbf{F} & (B \supset C) \supset (A \supset C)\ \checkmark \\ \textbf{T} & B \supset C\checkmark \\ \textbf{F} & A \supset C\ \checkmark \\ \textbf{T} & A \\ \textbf{F} & C \end{array}$$

This tableau has hit a contradiction in all the branches. So all cases where the sentence (of the first line) is false are contradictory. This means that the sentence $(A \supset B) \supset [\,(B \supset C) \supset (A \supset C)\,]$ cannot be false. By indirect proof it is a tautology.

Doing this with truth tables would have taken a lot longer, and would not have been so clear.

Here is the tableau method applied to another sentence.

$$\sim(A \cdot B) \supset (\sim A \vee \sim B)$$

We know that this sentence is a tautology (see page 75). If we assume it to be false, we should hit a contradiction:

$$\textbf{F}\quad \sim(A \cdot B) \supset (\sim A \vee \sim B)$$

Because the main connective is a material implication, we know that for the whole thing to be false the antecedent MUST be true and the consequent MUST be false.

$$\begin{array}{ll} \textbf{F} & \sim(A \cdot B) \supset (\sim A \vee \sim B)]\ \checkmark \\ \textbf{T} & \sim(A \cdot B) \\ \textbf{F} & \sim A \vee \sim B \end{array}$$

In the second line there is a negation that is true, since the only way a negation can be true is if the negated sentence is false, we can bring this down:

$$\begin{array}{ll} \textbf{F} & \sim(A \cdot B) \supset (\sim A \vee \sim B)]\ \checkmark \\ \textbf{T} & \sim(A \cdot B)\ \checkmark \\ \textbf{F} & \sim A \vee \sim B \\ \textbf{F} & A \cdot B \end{array}$$

The last two lines are respectively a false disjunction and a false conjunction. Either could be brought down, however we choose to bring the one that only has one possibility; that is, we bring down the one that does not branch (this is to lower the workload). There is only one way a disjunction can be false whereas there are many ways a conjunction can be false; look at the truth tables:

∨	A	B
T	T	T
T	T	F
T	F	T
F	F	F

The only row where the ∨ is false.

·	A	B
T	T	T
F	T	F
F	F	T
F	F	F

The rows where the · is false.

We will bring down the false disjunction first. From the truth tables we see that the only way a disjunction (∨) can be false is if both the sentences it connects are false.

$$
\begin{array}{ll}
\textbf{F} & \sim(A \cdot B) \supset (\sim A \vee \sim B)] \;\checkmark \\
\textbf{T} & \sim(A \cdot B) \;\checkmark \\
\textbf{F} & \sim A \vee \sim B \;\checkmark \\
\textbf{F} & A \cdot B \\
\textbf{F} & \sim A \\
\textbf{F} & \sim B
\end{array}
$$

We can now bring down the two new false negations we have generated:

$$
\begin{array}{ll}
\textbf{F} & \sim(A \cdot B) \supset (\sim A \vee \sim B)] \;\checkmark \\
\textbf{T} & \sim(A \cdot B) \;\checkmark \\
\textbf{F} & \sim A \vee \sim B \;\checkmark \\
\textbf{F} & A \cdot B \\
\textbf{F} & \sim A \;\checkmark \\
\textbf{F} & \sim B \;\checkmark \\
\textbf{T} & A \\
\textbf{T} & B
\end{array}
$$

Now there is only one thing left un-ticked, we have to bring down the conjunction. A conjunction is false when either one of the sentences it connects is false, or both. Because all "or"s are inclusive we can say that either one of the connected sentences is false or the other is; this includes the possibility of both being false. We write this using two branches:

$$\begin{array}{ll}
\mathbf{F} & \sim(A \cdot B) \supset (\sim A \vee \sim B)] \;\checkmark \\
\mathbf{T} & \sim(A \cdot B) \;\checkmark \\
\mathbf{F} & \sim A \vee \sim B \;\checkmark \\
\mathbf{F} & A \cdot B \\
\mathbf{F} & \sim A \;\checkmark \\
\mathbf{F} & \sim B \;\checkmark \\
\mathbf{T} & A \\
\mathbf{T} & B
\end{array}$$

$$\diagup \qquad \diagdown$$

$$\mathbf{F}\ A \qquad \mathbf{F}\ B$$
$$\times \qquad\quad \times$$

Either A is false. . .   . . . or B is.

In both branches since there is both a contradiction and nothing left to bring down, it is contradictory for the sentence $\sim(A \cdot B) \supset (\sim A \vee \sim B)$ to be false.

It is quite a common mistake, when faced with a tableau, to think you must put a contradiction on every letter. This is not true. A sentence is a tautology when, *on every branch, at least one letter* contradicts itself (not necessarily the same letter).

If the sentence is not a tautology, we should be able to bring down all the sentences and not hit a contradiction on *at least one of the branches*. If this happens this sentence can be false, so it is not a tautology (as it could be false). Consider this sentence:

$$[\,A \supset (B \supset C)\,] \supset [\,(C \supset B) \supset (C \supset A)\,]$$

If you have a particularly keen eye for this sort of thing then you will see that the sentence is not a tautology.

First of all we assume the sentence to be false:

$$\mathbf{F} \quad [\,A \supset (B \supset C)\,] \supset [\,(C \supset B) \supset (C \supset A)\,]$$

The main connective is a material implication, and there is only one way that that can be false.

$$\begin{array}{ll}
\mathbf{F} & [\,A \supset (B \supset C)\,] \supset [\,(C \supset B) \supset (C \supset A)\,] \;\checkmark \\
\mathbf{T} & A \supset (B \supset C) \\
\mathbf{F} & (C \supset B) \supset (C \supset A)
\end{array}$$

The next line to bring down is the third one, as there is only one way a material implication can be false and three in which it can be true (though in a tableau we can express this in two branches). Remember that you are not wrong to bring down branching lines first; you are just giving yourself more work.

F $[A \supset (B \supset C)] \supset [(C \supset B) \supset (C \supset A)]$ $\checkmark$
T $A \supset (B \supset C)$
F $(C \supset B) \supset (C \supset A)$ $\checkmark$
T $C \supset B$
F $C \supset A$

Once again we bring down the false material implication as it is simpler.

F $[A \supset (B \supset C)] \supset [(C \supset B) \supset (C \supset A)]$ $\checkmark$
T $A \supset (B \supset C)$
F $(C \supset B) \supset (C \supset A)$ $\checkmark$
T $C \supset B$
F $C \supset A$ $\checkmark$
T C
F A

Now we have two lines left un-ticked (we have not used them). We could bring either down, I choose to bring the $C \supset A$ down because it is smaller:

F $[A \supset (B \supset C)] \supset [(C \supset B) \supset (C \supset A)]$ $\checkmark$
T $A \supset (B \supset C)$
F $(C \supset B) \supset (C \supset A)$ $\checkmark$
T $C \supset B$ $\checkmark$
F $C \supset A$ $\checkmark$
T C
F A

F C **T** B
 ×

There is a contradiction on one branch so we need not do any more work on it. We must bring down the only line left un-ticked. In this sentnece the antecedent is A and the consequent is $B \supset C$. We bring it down with the A in one branch and the $B \supset C$ in the other branch.

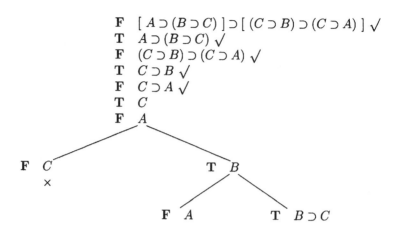

There are two branches now that do not have contradictions in them. If you look at the left one (the one with the **F** A at the end) you will see that there is no line in it that has not been ticked.[5] We have found a complete branch with no contradiction in it, so we could stop here, but I will continue anyway.

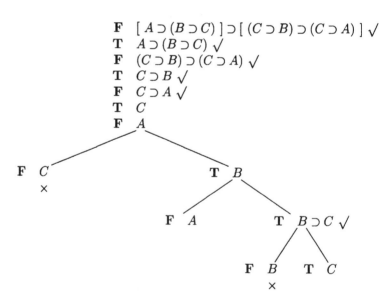

There is a contradiction on every branch except two. The sentence could be false, which means that it is not a tautology.

Here is what the tableau would look like if we had brought all the branching lines down first:

---

[5]Start at the very bottom, the **F** A. Then follow the branch upwards, you are not allowed to go down again. You will see that you never pass an un-ticked line (except for lines which are just one letter, but these do not count as you cannot break them up any more).

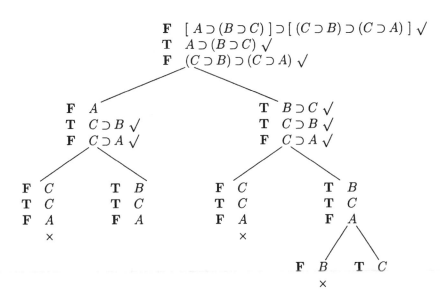

I shall not go into the mechanics of how this tableau was derived for the simple reason that it is a waste of space and you should be able to work it out yourself. What is important is that the truth values of the letters in the branches without contradictions are the same in both tableaux. This illustrates that it does not matter which way round you bring them down, you still get the same answer.

Here is an easy way to check if your tableau has produced a correct result when it says a sentence is not a tautology. Look at the columns without contradictions and read the truth values of the letters in them. Plug these truth values into a truth table and see if the sentence comes out false.

If we look up the non-contradictory columns in the last example we see that they give the same truth values to all the letters: **F** A, **T** B, and **T** C. Let us put these into a truth table and see if it comes out all right.

$$[\quad A \quad \supset \quad (B \quad \supset \quad C) \quad] \quad \supset \quad [\quad (C \quad \supset \quad B) \quad \supset \quad (C \quad \supset \quad A) \quad]$$
$$ F \quad T \quad T \quad T \quad T \quad F \quad\quad T \quad T \quad T \quad F \quad T \quad F \quad F$$

We have found a situation in which the sentence is false. Note that this method will not tell you whether you have made a mistake in your tableau, only that it has produced some correct results.[6]

Here are some more sentences:

$$(A \cdot B) \supset [C \supset (A \lor B)]$$

---

[6]It is possible to get the right answer from thoroughly incorrect working which, as any good maths teacher will tell you, is just as bad if not worse than simply getting it wrong.

Read this out loud and try to work out what it might mean. Do you think it is a tautology? First we assume that the sentence is false.

$$\textbf{F} \quad (A \cdot B) \supset [\, C \supset (A \lor B)\,]$$

There is only one way a material implication can be false (the main connective is a material implication), so we bring this straight down with no branching.

$$
\begin{array}{ll}
\textbf{F} & (A \cdot B) \supset [\, C \supset (A \lor B)\,] \; \checkmark \\
\textbf{T} & A \cdot B \\
\textbf{F} & C \supset (A \lor B)
\end{array}
$$

Neither of the two sentences that are un-ticked are ones that are going to branch. We know that a false material implication will not branch. A true conjunction (second line) will also not branch, as there is a conjunction is true if and only if both the conjuncts are true. Since it does not matter which we bring down first, I will bring down the conjunction.

$$
\begin{array}{ll}
\textbf{F} & (A \cdot B) \supset [\, C \supset (A \lor B)\,] \; \checkmark \\
\textbf{T} & A \cdot B \; \checkmark \\
\textbf{F} & C \supset (A \lor B) \\
\textbf{T} & A \\
\textbf{T} & B
\end{array}
$$

Now we have to bring down the false material implication.

$$
\begin{array}{ll}
\textbf{F} & (A \cdot B) \supset [\, C \supset (A \lor B)\,] \; \checkmark \\
\textbf{T} & A \cdot B \; \checkmark \\
\textbf{F} & C \supset (A \lor B) \; \checkmark \\
\textbf{T} & A \\
\textbf{T} & B \\
\textbf{T} & C \\
\textbf{F} & A \lor B
\end{array}
$$

All that is left to bring down is the false disjunction. A disjunction is false only when both the disjuncts are false (look at the truth table) so there will be no branching in this tableau.

$$
\begin{array}{ll}
\textbf{F} & (A \cdot B) \supset [\, C \supset (A \lor B)\,] \; \checkmark \\
\textbf{T} & A \cdot B \; \checkmark \\
\textbf{F} & C \supset (A \lor B) \; \checkmark \\
\textbf{T} & A \\
\textbf{T} & B \\
\textbf{T} & C \\
\textbf{F} & A \lor B \\
\textbf{F} & A \\
\textbf{F} & B \\
& \times
\end{array}
$$

The sentence is a tautology. Note that, in one column in this tableau, two letters were involved in contradictions. This makes no difference: one contradiction is just as good as two (on the same branch, that is).

Here is another sentence.

$$[A \supset (\sim B \vee C)] \supset [A \cdot (B \supset C)]$$

First we assume it to be false:

F $[A \supset (\sim B \vee C)] \supset [A \cdot (B \supset C)]$

Next we write down the antecedent as true and the consequent as false (the only way the main connective can be false since it is a material implication).

F $[A \supset (\sim B \vee C)] \supset [A \cdot (B \supset C)]$ $\checkmark$
T $A \supset (\sim B \vee C)$
F $A \cdot (B \supset C)$

Both of the next two lines branch, so it makes no difference at all which we bring down. I will bring down the material implication because I feel like it.

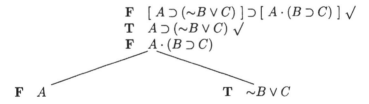

We now have two sentences to bring down. It will involve less work if we bring down the false conjunction on line three as that will drop to both branches. The true conjunction at the bottom right of the tableau drops only to the right branch as it is on only the right branch. As a rule, when you drop a sentence, it will only drop to the branches that are directly below it; it does not drop to a branch that started above it. Remember that when you do drop a sentence, it drops to *all* the branches that are below it (those that stem from the branch of that sentence).

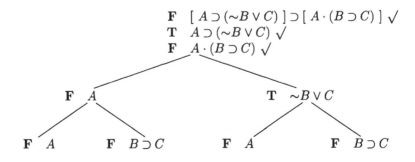

The branch on the far left has no un-ticked lines above it and there is no contradiction there; this means that the whole sentence will be false when A is false regardless of what truth values the other two take. If A is false, then $A \supset (\sim B \vee C)$ is true and $A \cdot (B \supset C)$ has to be false; the former is the antecedent, the latter is the consequent (of the main connective which is a material implication). Technically, because we have found a branch with no contradiction, we can stop here. However I will finish the tableau.

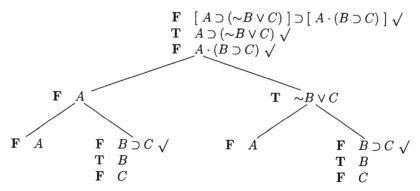

Let us add the last two steps in one go (the $\sim B$ on the bottom right).

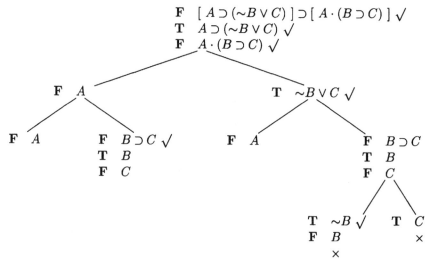

There are some branches in the tableau in which there are contradictions, so the sentence is *not necessarily false*. Here is the tableau for one that is.

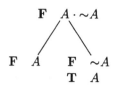

We know that $A \cdot \sim A$ is a contradiction, that is why the sentence $\sim(A \cdot \sim A)$ is a tautology. Notice that all (both) of the branches had no contradictions in them.

Fact 6.2.1 *If in a tableau for a sentence, all the branches contain a contradiction then the sentence is a tautology; otherwise it is not.*

At this point, you may think that a tableau with no contradictions at all means that the sentence itself is a contradiction. We have not given enough tableau rules for saying this. Consider the sentence A, when we write the tableau for this we do not have any contradictions, however the sentence A is certainly not a contradiction.[7]

6.2.1 The rules of the tableau

Here is a complete list of the tableau rules. The top line of each section is what you might have to bring down – for example a true negation. The bottom lines are what it is brought down as.

---

[7]The rule you need to add to make things work is as follows. A sentence can be said to be contradictory when no branch on the tableau is contradictory and there are at least 2^n different branches, where n is the number of different letters in the original sentence, not counting the same letter turning up more than once.

Negation

T	$\sim A$		F	$\sim A$
F	A		T	A

Conjnction

T	$A \cdot B$		F	$A \cdot B$
T	A			
T	B		F A	F B

Disjunction

T	$A \vee B$		F	$A \vee B$
T A	T B		F	A
			F	B

Material Implication

T	$A \supset B$		F	$A \supset B$
F A	T B		T	A
			F	B

A copy of these tableau rules is in Appendix A. Use it as a reference guide if you ever forget what to do.

6.3   Exercises

Use the tableau method to determine whether the following are tautologies. State your conclusion.

1. $(A \supset B) \supset [(A \supset (B \supset C)) \supset (A \supset C)]$

2. $\sim[(A \vee B) \supset C] \supset [\sim(A \supset C) \vee \sim(B \supset C)]$

3. $[(A \vee B) \supset \sim C] \supset [\sim(A \supset C) \cdot \sim(B \supset C)]$

4. $[(A \supset B) \cdot (B \supset C)] \supset [(C \supset D) \supset (\sim D \supset \sim C)]$

5. $[(A \cdot (B \supset C)] \supset [B \supset (A \cdot C)]$

6. $[(A \cdot B) \supset C] \supset [A \supset (B \supset C)]$

7. $[A \supset (B \supset C)] \supset [(A \cdot B) \supset C)]$

8. $\sim[A \supset (B \cdot C)] \supset [A \cdot (\sim B \vee \sim C)]$

9. $[(A \supset C) \cdot (B \supset D)] \supset [(A \vee B) \supset (C \vee D)]$

10. $B \supset [(A \cdot (A \supset B)) \vee (\sim A \cdot (\sim A \supset B))]$

6.4 The way of the tableau for validity

Now we come to do what we have been aiming for: we can use our propositional logic to find validity in long complicated arguments. Essentially we treat the argument the same way we did with truth tables, except we do not need to rewrite the argument as a sentence. Let us try this out on the already familiar Modus Ponens:

$$A$$
$$\underline{A \supset B}$$
$$B$$

First, assume that the premises are true and the conclusion false; then try to derive contradictions on all branches (if it cannot be that the premises are true and the conclusion false then the argument is valid).

$$\textbf{T} \quad A$$
$$\textbf{T} \quad \underline{A \supset B}$$
$$\textbf{F} \quad B$$

Now there is only the $A \supset B$ to bring down. If you look at the previous page, you will see that a true material implication branches like this:

$$
\begin{array}{ll}
\textbf{T} & A \\
\textbf{T} & A \supset B \;\checkmark \\
\textbf{F} & B
\end{array}
$$

$$
\begin{array}{cc}
\textbf{F}\;A & \textbf{T}\;B \\
\times & \times
\end{array}
$$

There are contradictions on every branch: Modus Ponens is definitely a valid argument which we have proved at least three different ways.[8]

See how quick this was. Compare this with the five lines we had to write when we used the truth table method.

Let us now prove some more arguments to be valid (or not). Here is the very useful Modus Tollens. First we assume the premises to be true and the conclusion to be false.

---

[8]In one of the greatest logic books of all time, Lewis Carrol pointed out in the conversation between Alice, the Griffin, and the Mock Turtle that in our arguments for Modus Ponens' validity we actually use Modus Ponens. Many philosophers use this as an example of how circularity is not necessarily a bad thing. We shall ignore this debate (see also the footnote on page 50)

$$
\begin{array}{ll}
\text{T} & \sim B \\
\text{T} & \underline{A \supset B} \\
\text{F} & \sim A
\end{array}
$$

To reduce the amount of work, we will bring down the negations first.

$$
\begin{array}{ll}
\text{T} & \sim B \ \checkmark \\
\text{T} & \underline{A \supset B} \\
\text{F} & \sim A \ \checkmark \\
\text{F} & B \\
\text{T} & A
\end{array}
$$

There is only one line left to bring down.

$$
\begin{array}{ll}
\text{T} & \sim B \ \checkmark \\
\text{T} & \underline{A \supset B} \ \checkmark \\
\text{F} & \sim A \ \checkmark \\
\text{F} & B \\
\text{T} & A
\end{array}
$$

$$
\begin{array}{cc}
\text{F } A & \text{T } B \\
\times & \times
\end{array}
$$

Again the tableau method is much simpler.

To finish, let us sum up everything we have done already by analysing an argument written in English:

> If Billy grows a beard, Dusty grows one as well, and if Dusty grows a beard, Frank either decides to leave the band or he grows a moustache. Billy has a beard. Frank is still in the band. Therefore Frank has a moustache.

We must translate this argument into propositional logic. It is quite clear that the first sentence can be rewritten: "If Billy has a beard then Dusty has a Beard."[9] The argument formalizes like this:

$$
\begin{array}{l}
A \supset B \\
B \supset (C \vee D) \\
A \\
\underline{\sim C} \\
D
\end{array}
$$

---

[9]There are people who would quibble about it being possible to have a beard without actually growing one due to ambiguities in the language. It is true that before you rewrite a sentence so that it translates more easily into propositional logic, you must make sure that the rewrite preserves the intended meaning.

Key
A = Billy has a beard
B = Dusty has a beard
C = Frank decides to leave the band
D = Frank grows a moustache

Now we bring down the negated C (after we have assumed the premises to be true and the conclusion to be false).

$$
\begin{array}{ll}
\textbf{T} & A \supset B \\
\textbf{T} & B \supset (C \lor D) \\
\textbf{T} & A \\
\textbf{T} & \sim C \checkmark \\
\textbf{F} & D \\
\textbf{F} & C
\end{array}
$$

Looking at the lines we have not yet brought down, you should be able to see that both of them will branch. I choose to bring the $A \supset B$ down first since one of its branches will have an **F** A in it; this will immediately generate a contradiction, thus reducing the workload.

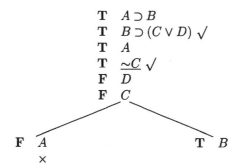

There is only one line left to bring down.

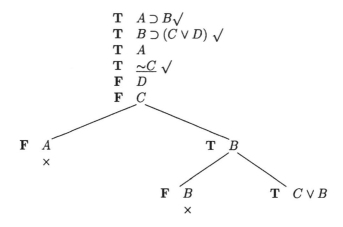

Finally we bring down the last un-ticked line (the $C \vee D$) in order to complete the tableau.

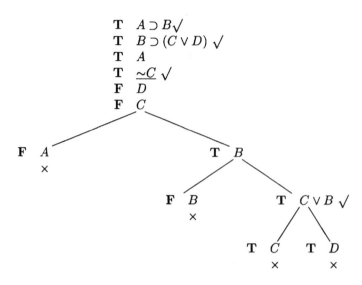

The argument is valid, and we have actually done something useful with our logic.

6.5   Exercises

Determine by the tableau method whether the following arguments are valid (because of the truth functions contained in them).

1. $(A \vee B)$
    $\underline{A \supset \sim B}$
    B

2. $A \supset (B \cdot C)$
    $B \supset \sim (C \vee D)$
    $\underline{D}$
    $\sim A$

3. $(A \vee B) \cdot C$
    $\underline{\sim A \cdot \sim C}$
    $B \vee D$

4. $A \supset (B \supset C)$
    $B \cdot \sim C$
    $\underline{D \supset \sim (\sim B \vee C)}$
    $A \supset \sim D$

$\sim A \vee (B \cdot \sim C)$
$\sim A \supset D$

5. $\sim D$
$\underline{C \vee E}$
$B \cdot E$

$(A \cdot B) \supset C$
$D \supset A$

6. $E \supset B$
$\underline{\sim C}$
$\sim A \vee \sim B$

$A \supset (B \vee \sim C)$
$(A \cdot C) \supset \sim D$

7. $\underline{C \supset (\sim B \vee D}$
$\sim A \vee \sim C$

$A \supset (B \vee \sim C)$
$(A \cdot C) \supset \sim D$

8. $\underline{C \supset (\sim B \vee D}$
$\sim A \vee \sim C$

$(A \vee B) \supset (C \cdot D)$

9. $\underline{(D \vee E) \supset (C \not\equiv A)}$
$\sim A$

$(A \supset C) \cdot (B \supset \sim C)$

10. $\underline{\sim [A \cdot (B \supset \sim D)]}$
$\sim C \vee \sim D$

Chapter 7

Propositional Logic: The Interesting Bits

7.1 What is so interesting?

We shall now derive an important result: that every sentence in propositional logic has a truth table, and every truth table has a sentence to go with it.

It is easy to see that there is a truth table for every sentence. We have spent whole chapters on how to build them. In the next section I will show that we can use only three truth functions to construct a sentence for every truth table. Then I will show how we can use only two and finally how we can use only one.

We have only defined five of the infinitely many truth functions of propositional logic: $\cdot$, $\lor$, $\supset$, $\equiv$ and $\sim$.

7.2 Only three truth functions are necessary

We can express material equivalence in terms of material implication and conjunction. Look at these truth tables.

(A	$\equiv$	B)		[(A	$\supset$	B)	$\cdot$	(B	$\supset$	A)	]
T	**T**	T		T	T	T	**T**	T	T	T	
T	**F**	F		T	F	F	**F**	F	T	T	
F	**F**	T		F	T	T	**F**	T	F	F	
F	**T**	F		F	T	F	**T**	F	T	F	

The formula on the left takes the same truth values as the formula on the right. Instead of using material equivalence ($A \equiv B$) we could write ($A \supset B$) $\cdot$ ($B \supset A$).[1] Material implication can also be expressed in terms of negation and disjunction, or negation and conjunction.

---

[1] Where A and B might be more complicated.

$$
\begin{array}{ccc}
A \supset B & \sim A \lor B & \sim (A \cdot \sim B) \\
\end{array}
$$

A	$\supset$	B	$\sim$	A	$\lor$	B	$\sim$	$(A$	$\cdot$	$\sim$	$B)$
T	**T**	T	F	T	**T**	T	**T**	T	F	F	T
T	**F**	F	F	T	**F**	F	**F**	T	T	T	F
F	**T**	T	T	F	**T**	T	**T**	F	F	F	T
F	**T**	F	T	F	**T**	F	**T**	F	F	T	F

The main connectives in all three sentences take the same truth values, this means that all three sentences are logically equivalent to each other. This shows that material implication is not necessary to express any sentence of Proposition Logic as, whenever we used $A \supset B$, we could have used $\sim A \lor B$ or $\sim(A \cdot \sim B)$ instead. So any sentence can be expressed using negation, conjunction and disjunction; or conjunction, material implication, and negation; or even material implication, negation, and disjunction.

Now I will show that any truth function can be written in terms of conjunction, negation, and disjunction. Consider this truth function:

$\star$	**A**	**B**	**C**
F	T	T	T
F	T	T	F
F	T	F	T
T	T	F	F
F	F	T	T
F	F	T	F
T	F	F	T
T	F	F	F

Can we find a sentence the main connective of which has the column of $\star$? Look at when $\star$ is true. It is true either when A is true, B is false, and C is false; or when A is false, B is false, and C is true, or when they are all false. The last sentence sums up the truth function perfectly. But if it sums up the truth function perfectly then, if we formalize it, we will get a sentence logically equivalent to that truth function. That is, if we write that long sentence in propositional logic we will have written out that truth function. To formalize that sentence is quite easy, here it is again:

> Either A is true, B is false, and C is false; or A is false, B is false, and C is true; or they are all false.

This formalizes quite simply to:

$$
\underbrace{(A \cdot \sim B \cdot \sim C)}_{\substack{A \text{ is true,} \\ B \text{ is false,} \\ C \text{ is false}}} \lor \underbrace{(\sim A \cdot \sim B \cdot C)}_{\substack{A \text{ is false,} \\ B \text{ is false,} \\ C \text{ is true}}} \lor \underbrace{(\sim A \lor \sim B \lor \sim C)}_{\substack{A \text{ is false,} \\ B \text{ is false,} \\ C \text{ is false}}}
$$

Check for yourself that it is correct. You will have to add brackkets to turn the triplets into pairs. Here is another:

★	A	B
T	T	T
F	T	F
F	F	T
T	F	F

This is true when either A is true and B is true or when both are false. We can write this as a sentence in propositional logic:

$$(A \cdot B) \vee (\sim A \cdot \sim B)$$

You may recognize this as material equivalence, which we have now expressed in terms of conjunction, disjunction, and negation. The procedure for constructing a sentence for any truth table is quite simple. You look at all the rows of the truth table for which the truth function is true (the way I have written it, that means all the Ts on the column on the far left). You then look at the truth values for the letters in that row and write a conjunction of the letters them, writing negations where you see an F. So, if there are three letters – the A column has a T, the B column has a T, and the C column has an F – you write this: "$A \cdot B \cdot \sim C$." You then join all the little sentences from each row into one long disjunction (remember to put brackets around each sentence).

Here is another truth function:

★	A	B	C
T	T	T	T
T	T	T	F
F	T	F	T
F	T	F	F
T	F	T	T
F	F	T	F
T	F	F	T
F	F	F	F

In the first row there is a T in the truth function column, so we look at the rest of that row and write down the following sentence (as all its letters' columns have Ts in them).

$$(A \cdot B \cdot C)$$

The second row also has a T in it; so we look over and see that the A is true, the B is true, but the C is false. We add to the previous sentence like this:

$$(A \cdot B \cdot C) \vee (A \cdot B \cdot \sim C)$$

The fifth row has a T in it also, so we add to it like this:

$$(A \cdot B \cdot C) \vee (A \cdot B \cdot \sim C) \vee (\sim A \cdot B \cdot C)$$

The seventh row also has a T in it.

$$(A \cdot B \cdot C) \vee (A \cdot B \cdot {\sim}C) \vee ({\sim}A \cdot B \cdot C) \cdot ({\sim}A \cdot {\sim}B \cdot C)$$

There are no more rows where the truth function is true so the above sentence expresses the truth table given above.

For a point of ease, suppose you have a truth table like this:

$\star$	A	B	C
T	T	T	T
F	T	T	F
T	T	F	T
T	T	F	F
T	F	T	T
T	F	T	F
T	F	F	T
F	F	F	F

This truth function is true a lot of the time, so any sentence we construct in the above way is going to be very long indeed. We can shorten it by saying when the sentence is not true, instead of saying when it is true. We look at all the rows with an F in them (there are only two) and write this as a conjuction of negations thus:

$${\sim}(A \cdot B \cdot {\sim}C) \cdot {\sim}({\sim}A \cdot {\sim}B \cdot {\sim}C)$$

This expresses the above truth table perfectly, check it for yourself. Look at this truth function:

$\star$	A	B
T	T	T
F	T	F
T	F	T
T	F	F

This has only one line with an F in it, so we can express it in one go.

$${\sim}(A \cdot {\sim}B)$$

Of course this is material implication.

7.3 Only two truth functions are necessary

There are many ways to do this, and we have already met one way above. All we have to show isthat we can express conjunction, negation, and disjunction using just two truth functions. Take a look at these truth tables.

	A	·	B		~	(A	⊃	~	B)		~	(~	A	∨	~	B)
	T	**T**	T		**T**	T	F	F	T		**T**	F	T	F	F	T
1.	T	**F**	F		**F**	T	T	T	F		**F**	F	T	T	T	F
	F	**F**	T		**F**	F	T	F	T		**F**	T	F	T	F	T
	F	**F**	F		**F**	F	T	T	F		**F**	T	F	T	T	F

	A	∨	B		~	A	⊃	B		~	(~	A	·	~	B)
	T	**T**	T		F	T	**T**	T		**T**	F	T	F	F	T
2.	T	**T**	F		F	T	**T**	F		**T**	F	T	F	T	F
	F	**T**	T		T	F	**T**	T		**T**	T	F	F	F	T
	F	**F**	F		T	F	**F**	F		**F**	T	F	T	T	F

	A	⊃	B		~	A	∨	B		~	(A	·	~	B)
	T	**T**	T		F	T	**T**	T		**T**	T	F	F	T
3.	T	**F**	F		F	T	**F**	F		**F**	T	T	T	F
	F	**T**	T		T	F	**T**	T		**T**	F	F	F	T
	F	**T**	F		T	F	**T**	F		**T**	F	F	T	F

(1) shows how we can express

conjunction in terms of material implication and negation, or disjunction and negation.

(2) shows how we can express

disjunction in terms of material implication and negation, or conjunction and negation.

(3) shows how we can express

material implication in terms of disjunction and negation or conjunction and negation.

We can take one of disjunction, conjunction or material implication and use it with negation to express all the other truth functions.

7.4 Only one truth function is necessary

7.4.1 Sheffer stroke

There does exist a truth function with which it is possible to express all other truth functions. One of them has an official name and symbol (though this is only true unofficially), and the others do not. Effectively what these truth functions do is combine one of disjunction, conjunction or material implication with negation into one truth function. Here is the truth table for Sheffer stroke; surprisingly it is denoted by a vertical stroke, so we get $A|B$.

Definition 7.4.1

|	A	B
F	T	T
T	T	F
T	F	T
T	F	F

This truth function is false when A and B are true and true otherwise. Anybody who has done any electronics will recognize this as the truth table for a NAND gate. This is because this truth table says "It is not the case that A and B" or "Either A is false or B is false" (remember that the "or" is inclusive). Here is how Sheffer stroke can be written in terms of the other truth functions.

```
 ~  (A   ·   B)        A  ⊃  ~  B         ~  A  ∨  ~  B
 F   T   T   T         T  F  F  T         F  T  F  F  T
 T   T   T   F         T  T  T  F         F  T  T  T  F
 T   F   T   T         F  T  F  T         T  F  T  F  T
 T   F   F   F         F  T· T  F         T  F  T  T  F
```

Sheffer stroke can express all the other truth functions, including negation, here is how:

```
 ~  A              A  |  A
 F  T              T  F  T
 T  F              F  T  F


 A  ·  B          (A  |  B)  |  (A  |  B)
 T  T  T           T  F  T   T   T  F  T
 T  F  F           T  T  F   F   T  T  F
 F  F  T           F  T  T   F   F  T  T
 F  F  F           F  T  F   F   F  T  F


 A  ∨  B          (A  |  A)  |  (B  |  B)
 T  T  T           T  F  T   T   T  F  T
 T  T  F           T  F  T   T   F  T  F
 F  T  T           F  T  F   T   T  F  T
 F  F  F           F  T  F   F   F  T  F
```

It is certainly not easy to get the hang of Sheffer stroke. Here is probably the best way to work out what the other truth functions look like in Sheffer stroke. Take conjunction: here is its truth table compared with the truth table of Sheffer stroke.

```
 A  ·  B          (A  |  B)
 T  T  T           T  F  T
 T  F  F           T  T  F
 F  F  T           F  T  T
 F  F  F           F  T  F
```

One is the negation of the other. Therefore if we write $\sim(A|B)$ then we will have written out conjunction. But we know how to write negation in terms of Sheffer stroke, so we can produce the whole sentence:

$$(A|B) \mid (A|B)$$

We could also do material implication from this but it would be rather complicated. Here is the Sheffer stroke version of material implication in its simplest form: $A|(B|B)$. This is obtained by writing the sentence $\sim(A \cdot \sim B)$ in terms of Sheffer stroke (remember that $A|B$ is logically equivalent to $\sim(A \cdot B)$. For the sceptics here is a truth table:

A	$\supset$	B		A	$\mid$	$(B$	$\mid$	$B)$
T	**T**	T		T	**T**	T	F	T
T	**F**	F		T	**F**	F	T	F
F	**T**	T		F	**T**	T	F	T
F	**T**	F		F	**T**	F	T	F

Sheffer stroke $(A|B)$ is also logically equivalent to the sentence $A \supset \sim B$ as that is logically equivalent to $\sim A \vee \sim B$.

It will not be too much of a shock to read that Sheffer stroke (also called *alternative denial*) is named after the mathematical logician who in 1913 first proved its ability to express all truth functions (although the logician Pierce had spotted this property some thirty years before).

7.4.2 Another sufficient truth function

There is another truth function that also has the property of being able to express any sentence in propositional logic. There is no official symbol for it so we can make up our own.[2] Here is a truth table:

Definition 7.4.2

$\heartsuit$	A	B
F	T	T
F	T	F
F	F	T
T	F	F

Electricians may recognize this as the truth table for the NOR gate. Because it has exactly the the truth conditions of $\sim(A \vee B)$. $\heartsuit$ translates nicely into English as "neither... nor...." Here is how the other truth functions are expressed using this truth function:

$\sim A$	$A \cdot B$	$A \vee B$	$A \supset B$
$A \heartsuit A$	$(A \heartsuit A) \heartsuit (B \heartsuit B)$	$(A \heartsuit B) \heartsuit (A \heartsuit B)$	$[(A \heartsuit A) \heartsuit B] \heartsuit [(A \heartsuit A) \heartsuit B]$

---

[2] Although $\downarrow$ is occasionally used.

Sheffer stroke and the truth function above are the only two binary truth functions that can alone express all truth tables. This can be easily (and tediously) shown by looking at all 16 possible truth tables for a binary connective. As an exercise, verify that all of these are correct using truth tables; if you feel like it, you can think up a more boring set of symbols to use (e.g. the $\downarrow$ symbol).

7.5   The big problem with propositional logic

7.5.1   Natural language is more than a few sentences

Propositional logic has one major drawback. As it stands, it is utterly incapable of dealing with syllogisms and arguments involving sentences like "All As are B." Consider the following very famous argument.

All men are mortal
<u>Socrates is a man</u>
Socrates is mortal

It would take a madman to say that this argument is invalid. However, according to propositional logic the argument is invalid, because the three sentences are different and cannot be related. The argument may as well be like this:

Billy is a pianist
<u>Joel is a singer</u>
The piano man is here

This argument is invalid, yet the analysis of it in propositional logic is the same as that for the Socrates argument. This is a big problem as we would like our logic to deal with any and all valid arguments. There are all sorts of clever tricks you can do with propositional logic to try and make it deal with these sentences; none of them are really any good. One way is to say that we should rewrite all our arguments like this:

All Men are mortal
<u>If all men are mortal then Socrates is mortal</u>
Socrates is mortal

This argument is valid, however, it is not quite the same as the original. For one thing the original argument implies that Socrates is a man; it expressly states it. This argument does not imply that Socrates is a man. You can add all sorts of things to make the two arguments equivalent until you get either an unsatisfactory result or an infinitely long sentence and an incorrect analysis of sentences involving the word "All" (think of a long conjunction of sentences: "A is mortal, B is mortal,..., Socrates is mortal, Eric Clapton is mortal, etc."). There still leaves these arguments to be dealt with.

All cats are mammals
<u>All mammals are vertebrates</u>
All cats are vertebrates

An argument with this structure, which seems to escape propositional logic completely, is called a syllogism. The theory of syllogisms has been around since Aristotle, whereas the first form of propositional logic was posited by Boole in the 1850s.

This is not the only problem that propositional logic has. Consider the following argument:

> All cats are mammals
> All cats' heads are mammals' heads

This is a perfectly valid argument, and it displays a type of reasoning for which there are many weird and wonderful names such as *inference by complex conception*. It is a commonplace inference, also sometimes called *the oblique syllogism*, however propositional logic says it is invalid (the premise and the conclusion are two separate sentences that cannot be related using propositional calculus).

7.6 Exercises

1. Construct a sentence, using only the truth functions $\sim, \cdot, \vee$ and the sentences $A, B,$ and C so that the constructed sentence has the truth values indicated in the left column for the truth-value combinations in the other columns.

	A	B	C
F	T	T	T
F	T	T	F
T	T	F	T
F	T	F	F
F	F	T	T
F	F	T	F
T	F	F	T
F	F	F	F

2. Express the truth function of question 1 using only $\cdot$ and $\sim$.

3. Construct a sentence, using only the truth functions $\supset$ and $\sim$ and the sentences A and B so that the constructed sentence expresses the truth functional sentence $A \cdot B$.

4. Construct a sentence, using only the truth functions $\supset, \sim$ and the sentences A and B so that the constructed sentence expresses the truth functional sentence $A \vee B$.

5. Express the truth functions $\sim, \vee,$ and $\cdot$ using only the truth function $|$ (Sheffer stroke) below.

$$
\begin{array}{ccc}
A & | & B \\
T & F & T \\
T & T & F \\
F & T & T \\
F & T & F
\end{array}
$$

Express the truth functions $\sim$, $\vee$ and $\cdot$ using only the truth function $\heartsuit$ belo

6.

$$
\begin{array}{ccc}
A & \heartsuit & B \\
T & F & T \\
T & F & F \\
F & F & T \\
F & T & F
\end{array}
$$

Chapter 8

Where Sheffer Can Put His Stroke

8.1   Everyone will have a stroke, eventually

Sheffer stroke is a pain, which causes problems for almost everybody. It has no intuitive natural language counterpart, and there is no apparent use for it. The only point to Sheffer stroke's existence seems to be that it exists. However it does have the curious property of being able to divide those who really can do abstract logic from those who cannot. Aside from remembering exactly what the truth table for it is, those who can play with Sheffer stroke confidently are the ones who can play with all other aspects of symbolic logic with an equal degree of confidence. Even the pointless and false things done about logic are useful in that they have been done. What is so useful about learning about Sheffer stroke is that it increases understanding of the logic and mastering Sheffer stroke entails a mastering of many other aspects of logic.

8.2   A shelf shuffling game

Imagine you have a stack of shelves, each of which has a see-through glass door that can be locked or unlocked. Here is a picture of these shelves:

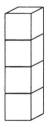

The shelves contain suits. Here is a picture of the shelves when they are full:

115

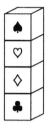

Each shelf may be locked or unlocked. All the shelves in the pictures above are unlocked. Here is what it looks like when all the shelves are locked:

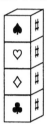

In the following picture the top two shelves are locked, but the bottom two shelves are unlocked:

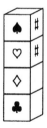

Here are two sets of shelves. On the left the bottom two shelves are locked, and on the right the top shelf and the second from the bottom shelf are locked:

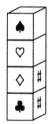   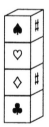

It should be clear that when a shelf is locked it has a ♮ sign on its side.

Now we are ready to play with these shelves. The shelves some peculiar properties. One is that all the locks are connected, so that if you unlock a particular shelf all the other locked shelves become unlocked as well, and all the shelves that are unlocked become locked. This will also happen if you lock one of the unlocked shelves. All of this can be put into a simple rule:

Rule 8.2.1 (Lock-reverse) If you apply the rule *lockrev* then all the locked shelves become unlocked and all the unlocked shelves become locked.

The following shows how *lockrev* may be applied.

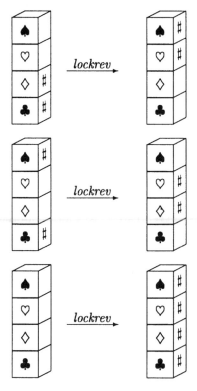

All *lockrev* does is reverse the locks on the shelves so that all the locked shelves become unlocked, and all the unlocked shelves become locked.

The designer of these shelves also allowed two more rules, which allow the physical movement of the shelves.

Rule 8.2.2 (Big-flipover) In *bigflip*, top two shelves are switched with the bottom two shelves.

Here are a few of examples of *bigflip* in action (remember that the locks move with the shelves).

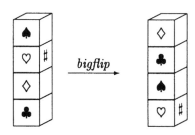

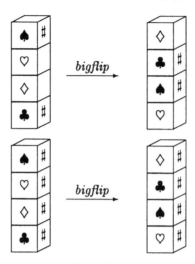

The next rule is slightly more complicated, but it is the last rule of the game. The shelves are on an ingenious ratchet system that allows you to do one more thing: you can switch the top two shelves for each other and at the same time swap the bottom two shelves for each other:

Rule 8.2.3 (Little-flipover) In *littleflip*, the top two switch positions and at the same time the bottom two shelves switch positions.

Here are a few examples of *littleflip* in action:

   The designer of the shelves has rigged everything so that all that can be done with these shelves is to follow the rules. Now we may start the game.

   The owner of the shelves, for reasons unknown, wants the locks on the shelves to be in a particular order. He does not care what order the objects inside the shelves are in; the only thing he cares about is the locks. The shelves start off with the locks in a particular order, and the object of the game is to use the rules to change the pattern of the locks to the one wanted by the owner. Here is an easy example:

The picture of the filled shelves on the left represents way the shelves really are, and the picture of the empty shelves on the right represents the way the owner wants the locks to be. It should be easy to see that if we apply *lockrev* then the locks will be in the order we want (remember that the owner does not care about the order of the things in the shelves).

That was quite an easy one. Here is another one:

This is slightly harder than the last one but (remembering that we have to make only the patterns of the locks match up) you should be able to see that in one step we can do it using *bigflip*:

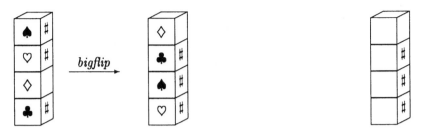

Some shelf-shuffles will need more than one operation. Here is one that will require two:

The first t   ʒ to notice about this one is that the starting shelf setup has three locked she   ‚, and the goal has only one. The first step should be obvious: we use *lockrev. lockrev* inverts the locks, so it will turn three locks into only one:

Now the next step. There are two to choose from (we can use a rule more than once but to apply *lockrev* again would be stupid). We want to move the lock that is at the second from the bottom shelf to the bottom shelf. *Bigflip* will move the lock to the second from the top shelf. So *littleflip* should do the trick.

It is utterly academic what is in the shelves, as we do not use them. The only reason they are there is to make it easier to see how the shelves are being moved around.

Exercises

On the left are the starting shelves and on the right are the goal patterns for the locks. Just fill in the middle (some will require three steps):

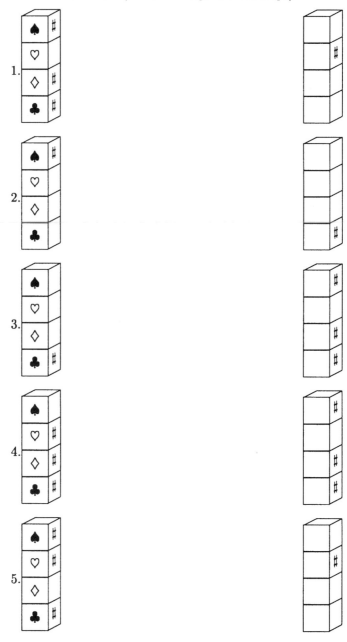

6. There are two different combinations of the locks for which applying the flip rules makes no difference in the pattern of the locks. What are they?

8.3   An interesting property of truth tables

Here is the truth table for a random truth function:

A	$\supset$	B
T	T	T
T	F	F
F	T	T
F	T	F

You should recognize it as the truth table for material implication. Let us see what happens when we put negation in various interesting parts of this table:

$\sim$	$(A$	$\supset$	$B)$
F	T	T	T
T	T	F	F
F	F	T	T
F	F	T	F

We have negated the entire formula. We know from basic logic that negation turns all Ts into Fs and all Fs into Ts. Here is another interesting place we can put the negation:

$(\sim$	A	$\supset$	$B)$
F	T	T	T
F	T	T	F
T	F	T	T
T	F	F	F

We have negated only the A. The main connective of the formula above is the $\supset$. Here is the column under $\supset$ in its truth table:

$$T$$
$$F$$
$$T$$
$$T$$

Here is the column under the $\supset$ when we negated only the A (the truth table for $\sim A \supset B$):

$$T$$
$$T$$
$$T$$
$$F$$

Here they are next to each other:

$$
\begin{array}{cc}
T & T \\
F & T \\
T & T \\
T & F
\end{array}
$$

They are exactly the same except the top two of one are the bottom two of the other. And the bottom two of one are the top two of the other (one has T, T at the top and T, F at the bottom, while the other has T, F at the top and T, T at the bottom).

Here is another interesting place we can put the negation:

$$
\begin{array}{cccc}
(A & \supset & \sim & B) \\
T & F & F & T \\
T & T & T & F \\
F & T & F & T \\
F & T & T & F
\end{array}
$$

Here is the truth table for $\supset$ and next to it is the column under the $\supset$ in the truth table above (the $\supset$ is the main connective).

$$
\begin{array}{cc}
T & F \\
F & T \\
T & T \\
T & T
\end{array}
$$

The only difference is that one has the top two truth values swapped over (as a matter of fact the bottom two truth values are swapped as well, but since they are both Ts it is not so obvious).

8.4 Back to the shelf game

It is very tiresome drawing these shelves all the time. I am now going to introduce a new and easier notation. We shall use the letter T to signify an open shelf and the letter F to signify a locked shelf (it does not matter to the game what is in the shelves, so we shall not bother introducing a notation for it). This is what it looks like when all the shelves are open:

$$
\begin{array}{c}
T \\
T \\
T \\
T
\end{array}
$$

this is what it looks like when all the shelves are locked:

$$
\begin{array}{c}
F \\
F \\
F \\
F
\end{array}
$$

This is what it looks like when the top shelf is open and all the other shelves are locked:

$$
\begin{array}{c}
T \\
F \\
F \\
F
\end{array}
$$

In the following, the bottom two shelves are locked, but the top two are open:

$$
\begin{array}{c}
T \\
T \\
F \\
F
\end{array}
$$

You should get the idea. Let us play the shelf game again using the new notation. The column on the left is the starting configuration of the locks on the shelves and the column on the right is the configuration we want to get to:

$$
\begin{array}{ccc}
T & & \boxed{\begin{array}{c} T \\ F \\ F \\ F \end{array}} \\
T & & \\
T & & \\
F & &
\end{array}
$$

Here is the solution:

T		F		F		T	T
T	*lockrev*	F	*bigflip*	T	*littleflip*	F	F
T		F		F		F	F
F		T		F		F	F

Exercises

Fill in the gaps.

1.

$$
\begin{array}{ccc}
T & & \boxed{\begin{array}{c} F \\ T \\ F \\ T \end{array}} \\
F & & \\
T & & \\
F & &
\end{array}
$$

2.

T T
F T
T F
T T

3.

F T
F T
F F
T T

4.

F T
T F
T F
F T

8.5 What's the connection?

The connection comes in three parts (exactly the same as the number of rules there are in the game)

Take any sentence written in logic that has the letters A and B in it, and write out its truth table. Look at the column under the main connective of the sentence, the one that tells you whether or not the sentence is a tautology (the final column you fill in when doing a truth table).

1. If you apply *lockrev* to that column then you will have the final column for the truth table of that entire sentence negated.

   So if you have $A \cdot (B \vee A)$ and you apply *lockrev* to the final column of its truth table you will get the final column of the truth table for $\sim [A \cdot (B \vee A)]$.

2. If you apply *bigflip* to that column then you will have the final column for the truth table of that sentence where all the As have been negated.

   So if you have $A \supset (A \vee B)$ and you apply *Bigflip* to the final column of its truth table you will get the final column of the truth table for $(\sim A) \supset ((\sim A) \vee B)$.

3. If you apply *littleflip* to that column then you will have the final column for the truth table of that sentence where all the Bs have been negated.

   So if you have $A \vee (\sim B)$ and you apply *littleflip* to the final column of its truth table you will get the final column of the truth table for $A \vee (\sim (\sim (B)))$ (which shortens to $A \vee B$).

It is important to note that these rules will only work under the condition that there are only two letters involved in the sentence for which we are producing truth tables. One more condition is that the truth table for the letters A and B are as follows:

A	B
T	T
T	F
F	T
F	F

That is, whenever you write a truth table you put the above columns under A and B (provided A and B are the only letters in the sentence of course). Can you see the significance of this condition?

8.6   Sheffer stroke

Sheffer stroke has the following truth table:

A			B
T	F	T
T	T	F
F	T	T
F	T	F

We are going to write the other truth functions in terms of Sheffer stroke by playing the shelf game; the starting configuration will be (the truth table for) Sheffer stroke, and the goal configuration will be the truth function we want to express. Let us do ⊃:

F	
T	
T	
T	
$A\|B$	

T
F
T
T
$A \supset B$

Underneath each truth table/shelf configuration is the formula that produces it. Now we can complete the shelf shuffle in one step, if we apply *littleflip*. So that is what we shall do. Above we said that *littleflip* is the same as negating all the Bs. We know how to write negation in terms of Sheffer stroke. If we want to negate a sentence, say A, using Sheffer stroke we write $A|A$. So when we apply *littleflip* in the example, we write underneath the new column the formula $A|B$ except that whenever we see a B we write $(B|B)$:

8.6. *8.6. SHEFFER STROKE* 127

F		T			T
T	littleflip	F			F
T		T			T
T		T			T
A|B		A|(B|B)			A ⊃ B

Here are the new extra rules for the shelf game:

1. When *lockrev* is applied, write twice underneath the new column the formula that is underneath the previous column, with a Sheffer stroke in the middle (in the middle of the two rewritten formulas).[1]

2. When *littleflip* is applied, write underneath the new column the formula that is underneath the previous column, except change all the *B*s to (*B*|*B*).

3. When *bigflip* is applied, write underneath the new column the formula that is underneath the previous column, except change all the *A*s to (*A*|*A*).

Here is how to derive the truth table for · using the shelf game:

F		T		T
T	lockrev	F		F
T		F		F
T		F		F
A|B		(A|B)|(A|B)		A · B

Exercises

1. Fill in the gaps and convert Sheffer stroke to get the truth table for ∨. You will need to do two operations.

F	T
T	T
T	T
T	F
A|B	A ∨ B

2. Do ∧, ∨, and ⊃ for the truth function ↓. All the rules are exactly the same except the starting configuration for the shelves is:

---

[1] That counts as negating the whole thing.

$$F$$
$$F$$
$$F$$
$$T$$
$$A \downarrow B$$

3. There are not enough rules to turn Sheffer stroke into any truth function. We cannot produce a truth table for material equivalence ($\leftrightarrow$) using only the current rules. Why?

4. Find a simple extra rule, together with how it changes formulas when applied, that is sufficient to turn Sheffer stroke into any truth function.

Hint: Try a rule that can change particular Ts and Fs in the table.

8.7   What we have just been doing

We have just been thinking about Sheffer stroke in terms of manipulating the patterns formed by its truth table. You may find it a lot easier to do logic if you think about all the truth functions in terms of patterns. It is much easier to think about logic when you are playing with something more real rather than with abstract entities such as a bunch of rules that have been written down for you. Try to think about logic in terms of applications of the rules rather than the rules themselves.

We have also gone part of the way towards finding a new way of understanding truth functions and their truth tables. We are used to thinking about classical propositional logic as the logic of truth, falsity, and sentences. It does not have to be. The above is what it might be like to use classical propositional logic as the logic of locks and strangely designed shelves. Logic is abstract so that it can be applied generally. The trick is to find an application of it that you can play with (and that works) and use that one. One good easy way is to think of it in terms of pattern manipulation.

Answers

Section 8.2

1. *lockrev*

2. *littleflip, bigflip*

3. *lockrev, bigflip*

4. *littleflip*

5. *lockrev, littleflip, bigflip*

6. Not telling. There are only sixteen different lock combinations; go through them all.

Section 8.4

1. *lockrev*

2. *bigflip, littleflip*

3. *lockrev, littleflip*

4. *lockrev.* Or, *bigflip.* Or, *littleflip.*

Section 8.6

1. *lockrev, littleflip, bigflip.* The sequence of formulas is: $A|B$, $A|(B|B)$, $(A|A)|(B|B)$.

2. Not telling.

3. Not telling.

4. *Hint*: Try a couple of rules that add ...$|A$ and ...$|B$ to the old formula ("..." is of course the old formula). Then see if you can reduce them to one rule.

Chapter 9

Syllogisms and Venn diagrams

9.1 The Syllogism

9.1.1 The Greeks' theory

Under Aristotle[1] – the first man to develop something vaguely resembling a formal logic – the syllogism was a very special sort of argument. It had to have two premises and a conclusion, each of which must be one of four possible types. The names I shall use for these types are not due to Aristotle but to logicians of the middle ages.

Definition 9.1.1

All x are y	*A form sentence*	*Universal affirmative*
Some x are y[2]	*I form sentence*	*Particular affirmative*
No x is y	*E form sentence*	*Universal negative*
Some x are not y	*O form sentence*	*Particular negative*

A syllogism is an argument involving two premises and a conclusion each of which is one of these types (but the full definition is more complex). Aristotle had a theory about how these work, one aspect of which was that all arguments can be reduced to them. One part of the quite ingenious theory that Aristotle produced is characterised by the *square of opposition* which looks like this:

---

[1] See the *Prior Analytics.*
[2] The "some" here means "there exists" as in "Some x is a y."

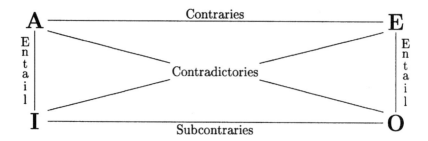

We can write a table for how the various forms of sentence interrelate.

	A	E	I	O
If **A** is true		False	True	False
If **A** is false		I/data[3]	I/data	True
If **E** is true	False		False	True
If **E** is false	I/data		True	I/data
If **I** is true	I/data	False		I/data
If **I** is false	False	True		True
If **O** is true	False	I/data	I/data	
If **O** is false	True	False	True	

This rather complicated and messy table can be summed up in a few rules.

1. An **A** form sentence and an **E** form sentence cannot both be true: $\sim(\mathbf{A}\cdot\mathbf{E})$ is a logical necessity.[4]

2. **I** and **O** cannot both be false: $\sim(\sim\mathbf{I}\cdot\sim\mathbf{O})$ is a logical necessity.

3. **A** entails **I**: $\mathbf{A}\supset\mathbf{I}$ is a logical necessity.

4. **E** entails **O**: $\mathbf{E}\supset\mathbf{O}$ is a logical necessity

5. **A** and **O** form sentences are contradictory, they cannot both be true or false: $\sim(\mathbf{A}\equiv\mathbf{O})$ is a logical necessity.

6. **E** and **I** are contradictory: $\sim(\mathbf{E}\equiv\mathbf{I})$ is a logical necessity.

9.1.2 The modern theory

The square of opposition has problems with rules (3) and (4). Does "All x are y" entail that there are any xs to be y? Likewise, does "No x is y" entail that there is an x that is not a y? Suppose there are no xs in existence, what do we say? If we follow Aristotle we cannot say that none of them are y or that all of them are y, whatever y may mean; as this implies that xs exist which, we have just supposed is not true. It would appear that Aristotle thought that we

---

[3]Insufficient data...captain.
[4]A sentence is a logical necessity when there is no way for it be false in logic (see Chapter 11).

should not say anything about something that does not exist. This may seem intuitive, but it is not very satisfactory as occasionally we make statements like this about things that do not exist. Here are some examples:

No evidence that flying pigs exist has been found.

This sentence is surely true. However there is certainly no implication that there actually exists evidence of flying pigs. Quite the contrary, if there is any implication then it is to the effect that there is no evidence of flying pigs. We could rewrite this sentence as:

Any evidence that flying pigs exist has not been found.

Is this sentence logically equivalent to the first one? If it is then just as before, it does not entail the existence of anything.

9.1.3 Formalising syllogisms

Some formal analysis of a syllogism is useful to know. Let us take a very general and open description of a syllogism:

x y
y z
—————
x z

This description leaves it open how you interpret what forms the sentences are. The syllogism could be like this for instance.

All x are y
All y are z
—————
Some x are z

Or it could be like this:

Some x are y
Some y are z
—————
No x is z

Look to the conclusion: the first letter (here the x) is called the *subject term* and the last letter (the z) is called the *predicate term*. The names carry through to the premises, so the x in the first premise is called the subject term, and in the second premise the z is called the predicate term. To tell the names of the letters you look at the order they appear in the conclusion. The y which appears in two of the premises is called the *middle term*; a middle term must appear in both premises for it to be called that. We can now put the final restriction on what is a syllogism: a syllogism must have a subject term, a predicate term, and a middle term.

Definition 9.1.2 *In a syllogism the term that appears first in the conclusion is called the* subject *term. The term which appears second in the conclusion is called the* predicate *term. The remaining term which appears in and only in both premises is called the* middle *term.*

S	M	
M	P	The conclusion of every syllogism
S	P	should have this structure.

The subject and predicate terms do not have to occur in the premises in that order:

S	M		M	S		M	S
P	M	or	M	P	or	P	M
S	P		S	P		S	P

Definition 9.1.3 *The figure of a syllogism is a matter of the order in which the S and the P appear in the premises. We are not going to bother with formalisations of all the possible figures of a syllogism as it complicates unnecessarily*

We may also add to our formalisation of syllogisms the letters (**A**, **E**, **I** or **O**) which signify the type of sentence. We may now analyze a syllogism like this:

All cats are mammals	**A**	S	M
All mammals are vertebrates	**A**	M	P
All cats are vertebrates	**A**	S	P

Remember that the M does not stand for mammals it stands for the middle term. It is just a fluke that they begin with the same letter.

No Greys have been seen	**E**	M	P
All Greys are aliens	**A**	M	S
Some aliens have not been seen	**O**	S	P

The last syllogism is an example of a case where Aristotelian logic and modern logic disagree. In Aristotelian logic the syllogism is valid as the two premises entail the existence of Greys and aliens. In modern logic this is not the case, for where there are no Greys or aliens, the premises are true and the conclusion is false.

Definition 9.1.4 *The* mood *of a syllogism is a matter of the form of each of the sentences that make up the syllogism. It is the combination of the* **A**, **E**, **I** *and* **O** *in the formalisation of the syllogism.*

There exists a formalisation naming each possible valid mood (with the appropriate figure) using of a lot of mnemonics. Learning them is a complete waste of time to be paralleled only with watching someone else play Solitaire. The important thing to remember here is that **A** and **E** form sentences ("All x are y" and "No x is y") do not imply the existence of anything whatsoever.

An interesting point is Aristotle's rather bold claim that all arguments can be reduced to a syllogism. For each syllogism there are $4^3 = 64$ possible moods. There are also four possible figures; this adds up to only $64 \times 4 = 256$ syllogisms. If Aristotle's claim were correct there would really be only 256 possible forms of argument.

9.2 Venn diagrams

All schoolchildren should have come across Venn diagrams at some point in their primary school education. Venn diagrams were the best thing to happen to mathematics and logic since the birth of Euclid.[5] They can be adapted to provide an intuitive and efficient system for doing almost anything you like.

Here is a simple Venn Diagram:

Classical Music   Good Music

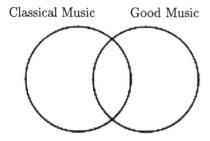

As the names suggest, the left circle represents all the classical music in existence, and the right circle represents all the good music in existence. Notice thaat these circles may be empty (there may be no classical or good music at all), it is left entirely open how you can fill them in. The Venn diagram above tells you absolutely nothing. All the classical music could be good, all the good music could be classical etc. We do not know from the diagram. Here is what we can add to these diagrams when we are given the sentences that make up a syllogism.

9.2.1 What to do with your Venn diagrams

The A form sentence

> All classical music is good.

This does not imply that there is any classical or good music; all it says is that there is no classical music that is not good. We can show this on our Venn diagram by shading out the area that represents the classical music that is not good music.

---

[5] Euler circles too. Pictures are always a good way of fathoming a difficult topic. To quote from the great book:

> "And what is the use of a book," thought Alice, "without pictures or conversation?"

Such thoughts hold true for any book or thought on any worthwhile subject whatsoever.

Classical Music   Good Music

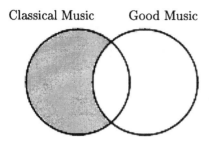

This Venn diagram says that all classical music is good music because the only part of the classical music circle that is shaded is not that part that is in the good music circle. *In a Venn diagram the areas of the parts are irrelevant; the sizes of the intersections or unshaded parts are not important.*

The E form sentence

No classical music is good.

This also does not imply anything about what sort of music available. All it says is that no classical music is good. We should shade out the intersection between the classical music circle and the good music circle.

Classical Music   Good Music

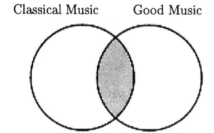

This Venn diagram now says that there is no classical music that is good (and that there is no good music that is classical).

The I form sentence

Some classical music is good.

This says something about the existence of classical music and good music. It is very easy to misread the word "some," here it does not mean less/fewer than half or the opposite of "most." Read "some" to mean that there exists at least one. So "some cats are mammals" should be read as: "there exists at least one cat that is a mammal." To deal adequately with quantifiers ("how much" words) like "most" and "some" in its other sense, we need a much more complex logical theory, something we shall ignore in this book.[6] Here is how we draw an I form sentence on a Venn diagram.

---

[6]People have tried to build logics to deal with these words ("a few," "most" etc.) using so called *fuzzy* set theory, associated with the famous *fuzzy logic*. This has been done with

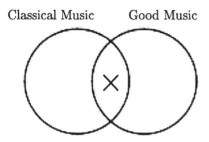

This Venn diagram says that there is a piece of classical music which is good, however, we do not know which or whether there are any more.

The O form sentence

> **Some classical music is not good.**

We treat this in exactly the same way as the last one, except that we put the cross in a different place.

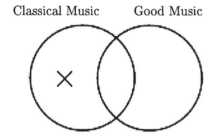

All this Venn diagram says is that there is a piece of classical music which is not good, it says nothing else.

9.2.2 Some intuition for Venn diagrams

Imagine someone is throwing darts at a Venn diagram shaped dartboard:

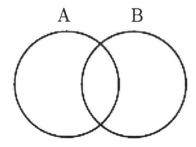

---

some degree of success, and fuzzy logics are used all over the place, from washing machines to stock market programs.

There are three ways to hit this dart-board: one could hit an A, a B, or the intersection and get both an A and a B. Suppose we modify the dartboard for a handicap and a **B**. Suppose someone is modifying the dart-board for a handicap game, according to various instructions (we cannot be bothered to build a new one).

Also, the dart players are perfect, so it does not matter how big the scoring areas are. Now picture what has to be done with the following sorts of instruction:

The A form sentence

All A hits will also B hits.

The A area must be blotted out so that only the intersection remains. We have only modified the dartboard; we do not know where any of the hits are going to land or if there are going to be any hits at all.

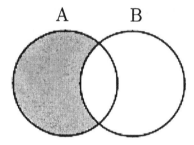

Now all the A hits will be B hits and the rest follows:

The O form sentence

Some A hit will not be a B hit

We have to cheat on behalf of one of the players as the command entails a hit being made. This means that we have to land at least one hit. Because we do not want to do too much work, we put in only one hit (one is enough to make it true that some of the hits land in the A but not in the B section). The hit is represented by a cross.

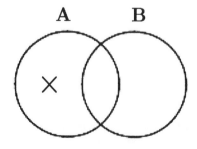

The reasoning behind the filling out of the Venn diagrams should be clear. It is very easy indeed to make a mistake when doing a Venn diagram if you are not absolutely certain what is going on.

9.3 Venn diagrams for validity

9.3.1 Three circle Venn diagrams

You should by now be able to quote the definition of validity in your sleep; as a matter of fact, everyone should be able to do that. An argument is valid if the conclusion is entailed by the premises (cannot be false if the premises are true). In a sense, the conclusion is contained in the premises if the argument is valid. For any syllogism we draw out a large Venn diagram and fill it in for the premises; if we can see that the conclusion has been filled in by filling out the premises then the argument is valid.[7]

A syllogism contains three terms: a subject term, a predicate term, and a middle term. Therefore we should draw three circles to represent each term. Note that each circle does not represent each sentence, but each term. Here is how to link the circles up for three.

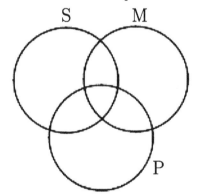

Where S stands for the subject term, M stands for the middle term and P stands for the predicate term. Here is how to analyze a syllogism using Venn diagrams. Consider the following argument:

All Syllogisms are three term arguments
All three term arguments use three circle Venn diagrams
All Syllogisms use three circle Venn diagrams

This argument takes a very familiar form:

A	S	M
A	M	P
A	S	P

---

[7]This does not entail that deduction tells us nothing new, merely that what is told is guaranteed by the premises.

There are three terms in this argument so we use a three circle Venn diagram. In this argument, the subject term is "syllogisms" and the predicate term is "three circle Venn diagrams" as they appear in that order in the conclusion. The middle term is what is left, namely "three term arguments."

Let us now fill in the Venn diagram according to the premises. We will do the first premise first. When filling in the Venn diagram, ignore the existence of the circles not mentioned in that premise. So this premise involves only S and M which means we should ignore the P circle. We fill in the Venn diagram like this:

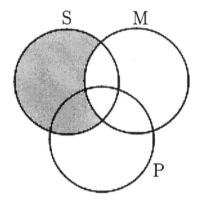

Now we fill in the next premise. This is also an **A** form sentence so we shall fill it in in much the same way. The premise is about M and P, so when filling out the diagram we ignore the S circle. The area we shall fill in is the area that represents all the Ms that are not P, since the premise says all M are P.

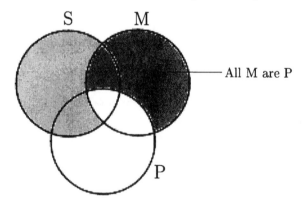

If we can read the conclusion from this diagram, it is valid. The conclusion is that all S are P. The part of the S circle which does not intersect with the P circle should be shaded. Looking at the diagram, this is exactly what has happened; as a matter of fact more has been shaded out. It does not matter if too much has been shaded out, even if it is the entire diagram. All that is important is that the area that, after filling out for the premises, the conclusion is already filled out.

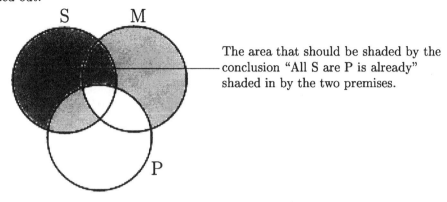

The area that should be shaded by the conclusion "All S are P is already" shaded in by the two premises.

As we can see, the conclusion can be read after filling in the two premises. This means that if they are true, the conclusion cannot be false: the argument is valid.

Here is another argument:

All Solitare games are pointless
Some pointless things are stupid
Some Solitare games are stupid

This argument also takes a familiar form (it is one of the classic invalid argument structures):

A	S	M
I	M	P
I	S	P

Despite the truth of all three sentences the argument is not valid. We will show this with a Venn diagram. It is best to do the universal first for reasons than will soon become apparent. The first premise is easy.

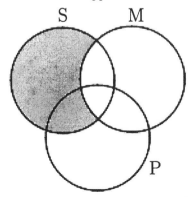

The next premise is not so easy; "Some M is P." Remember we did this by putting a cross in the intersection between M and P.

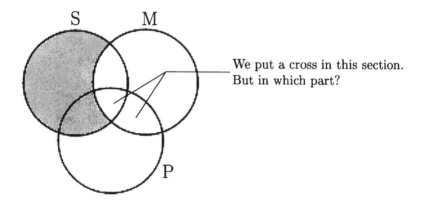

We put a cross in this section.
But in which part?

We do not have enough information to say where to put the cross. Previously I wrote that when doing one premise you may ignore the other circle not mentioned in that premise (in this case the S circle). Unfortunately that does not include those unshaded parts of the third circle which are within the two circles you are currently dealing with. When we have a situation in which a cross could be put in more than one area, we draw put on the line that separates the two possible areas; there will always be such a line. So we proceed like this.

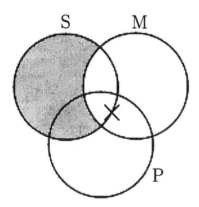

Can we read the conclusion from this Venn Diagram? The answer is no. The conclusion – some S are P – requires there to be a cross in the intersection between the S circle and the P circle.

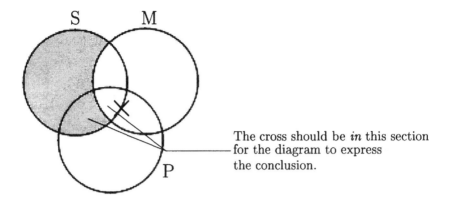

The cross should be *in* this section for the diagram to express the conclusion.

It is true that the cross is on the edge of one of the spaces in which the conclusion would put it, but that is not good enough. The cross has to be inside the intersection between S and P, because it is not, the argument is invalid; the conclusion cannot be read from the premises.

It is a good idea to do the universal sentences first because they blot out whole spaces in the Venn diagram. This may allow a cross to be put in a space rather than on a line between two spaces (if one is blotted out).

I	S	M
A	M	P
I	S	P

Look up what the letters mean at the start of the chapter (Def 9.1.1) if you cannot remember what they mean. First we shall fill in the extremely familiar **A** form premise; note that the terms involved are the M and the P, so we ignore the S circle.

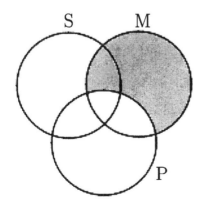

There is only one premise left – some S are M. There are two possible spaces for where the cross should go as the sentence is a particular (**I** form in this case).

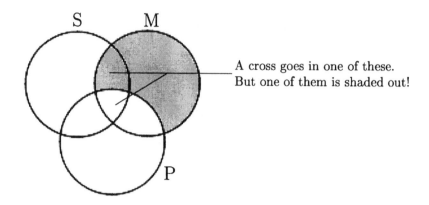

A cross goes in one of these. But one of them is shaded out!

One of the two possible spaces is shaded out, so in effect it does not exist. There is only one place the cross can go: not on any lines but in the middle.

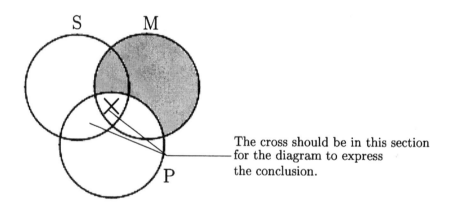

The cross should be in this section for the diagram to express the conclusion.

Now we can see that the conclusion "Some S are P" can be read from this Venn diagram. The conclusion puts a cross in the intersection between the S and the P, in more or less the same spot where there actually is a cross. The fact that there is across in the right place means that the conclusion can be read from the premises. This means that the argument is valid.

Here are some more:

E	M	P		No M is P
O	M	S		Some M is not S
I	S	P		Some S is P

The first premise is a universal so we shall do that one first.

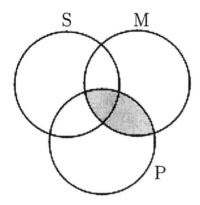

The second premise, is about M and P. The cross should go in the part of the M circle that is not in the S circle, but that area is divided, so the cross goes on the line between them. However, one of these areas is blotted out, so we should put the cross fully in the other area.

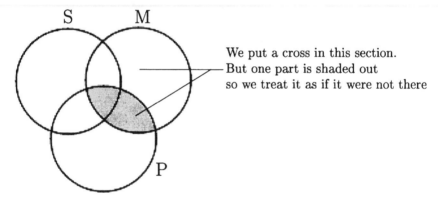

We put a cross in this section. But one part is shaded out so we treat it as if it were not there

The cross goes like this:

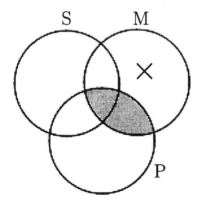

Can we read the conclusion from this Venn diagram? The answer is that we cannot. The conclusion would put a cross in the intersection between the S circle and the P circle:

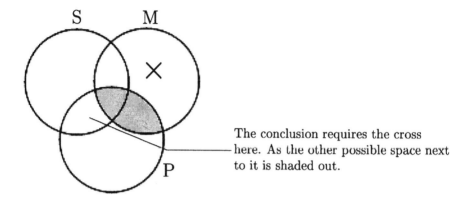

The conclusion requires the cross here. As the other possible space next to it is shaded out.

The argument is therefore invalid. Here is another:

O	S	M
A	P	M
O	S	P

We will do the universal premise first:

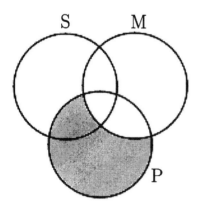

Now the second premise. We should be drawing a cross somewhere. It says that some S is not M, so we should put the cross in the part of the S circle that is not in the M circle.

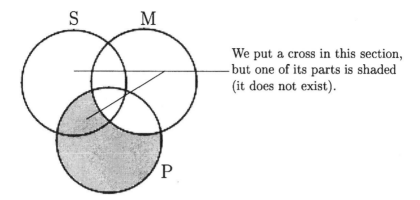

We put a cross in this section, but one of its parts is shaded (it does not exist).

Part of the S circle is shaded, so we do not put the cross on the line. When we put a cross on a line, we are saying that it could be in one side or in the other or even both, but we do not know which. A cross on a line is not enough because in a formal deduction you must be absolutely certain about everything.

In this example the cross goes like this:

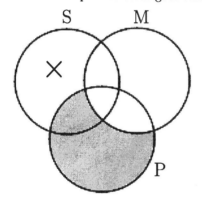

Can we read off the conclusion? The conclusion is that some S is not P. The cross is certainly in the right place, in the middle of the S circle that does not intersect with the P circle. The argument is valid.

You may have noticed already that there are considerably many more ways of producing an invalid argument than there are of producing a valid one. This is a standard law of nature from which Murphy's Law gets its empirical backing:, there are always many more ways something can go wrong compared to the number of ways it can go right. There is also only one correct way of doing a Venn diagram, and lots of ways of making a mistake; be very careful.

9.3.2 Venn and Aristotle

If, like Aristotle, you do not like the idea of the lack of existential implications in the universal sentences, then Venn diagrams can accommodate you. Here is how an **A** form sentence with existential implications

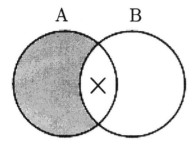

This Venn Diagram says that all A are B and that there is at least one A around (which we know is a B, which is why the cross is not on the line).

Some people believe that the Aristotelian system, where universals imply existence, is more intuitive and closer to natural reasoning. Certainly they have a case for positive universal sentences like the famous "All cats are mammals," but see the discussion of Section 9.1.2 for a serious problem eith negative universal sentences.

9.4   Problems with Venn diagrams

Venn diagrams are pictorial and hence bulky and very messy to use at times. Despite their problems they provide a unique insight into the workings of syllogisms, provided of course you understand what a Venn diagram is. I shall now outline a few problems with Venn diagrams as a general system for dealing with the validity of arguments.

9.4.1   Complicated arguments can be difficult to draw

Venn diagrams can deal efficiently only with arguments using three terms. Consider the following obviously valid argument.

A	A	B
A	B	C
A	C	D
A	A	D

Read it out aloud in translated form (see Def 9.1.1) if you cannot see its validity. Now try drawing a Venn diagram in which your four domains (circles or whatever shape you feel like using) intersect with each other in the 15 possible combinations necessary. Here is what a four term Venn Diagram could look like:

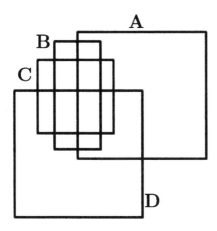

I shall not bother to show how this works, as it would be a waste of time and you should be able to work it out yourself. If a four-term Venn diagram (Venn diagram in its loosest possible sense) is this messy, imagine how complicated a five-term diagram will be.[8]

9.4.2 Venn diagrams cannot do truth functions

Venn diagrams cannot handle combinations of truth function and syllogism:

> If P then all A are B
> If Q then some A is not B
> ―――――――――――――――
> If Q then it is not the case that P

This is obviously a valid argument, but Venn diagrams alone cannot deal with it.

Venn diagrams are incapable of dealing with the following sort of argument, which propositional logic cannot deal with either:

> All cats are mammals
> ―――――――――――――
> All cats' heads are mammals' heads

Nor can they deal with this very famous form of argument:

> All men are mortal
> Socrates is a man
> ―――――――――――
> Socrates is mortal

Or even this:

> All the world loves a lover
> Romeo loves Juliet
> ―――――――――――
> Iago loves Desdemona

---

[8]As a matter of fact, in only two dimensions a general five-term Venn diagram is topologically impossible. Three dimensions are required. Or have a two dimensional diagram but were some overlaps occur more than once (e.g. an overlap of *only* A and B occurs twice).

The last argument is valid in a pedantic sort of way. If you cannot see why look to Section 11.5.2.

9.5   Exercises

By using Venn diagrams determine whether the following syllogisms are valid.

1. All candidates are teetotallers
    No teetotaller is happy
    No candidate is happy

2. Some students play tennis
    Some students do not play badminton
    Some tennis players do not play badminton

3. All intellectuals are philosophers
    No politician is a philosopher
    No politician is an intellectual

4. Only logicians are clever
    Some mathematicians are logicians
    Some mathematicians are clever

5.
E	S	M
O	P	M
O	S	P

6.
A	M	S
O	M	P
O	S	P

Chapter 10

Predicate Logic: On Natural Language

The question remains: how can we deal with those arguments that escaped both Venn diagrams and propositional logic? For example:

All men are mortal
<u>Socrates is a man</u>
Socrates is mortal

Humanity had to wait a couple of millennia after Aristotle before such a system called *predicate logic* was developed. It is also hear referred to as *First order predicate logic with identity* (if it includes the contents of section 11.7). It has also been given the name *classical quantifier calculus with identity* often abbreviated to CQC=, and *predicate calculus*.[1] The German mathematician and logician Gottlob Frege (1848-1925) developed predicate logic as a logic for doing mathematics and set theory. One of the main lines of attack against Predicate logic as a system of argument analysis is that it is designed only for mathematics and is unsuitable for common arguments.

10.1 Names and Predicates

Take any sentence that contains no truth functions. Here is a simple one:

Richard is a carpenter

Predicate logic divides sentences up into *names* and *predicates*. In the above sentence the name is "Richard." A name is a label that singles out a particular object. The predicate is the rest of the sentence that is not the name – ...is a carpenter. Sentences like "Richard is a carpenter" or "Debbie likes Denis" are

---

[1] You will also hear propositional logic referred to as *propositional calculus*.

called *basic* or *atomic* sentences. Atomic sentences do not contain any truth functions.

A comprehensive definition of a name that avoids deep logical theory is not quite so easy to give. However here, is a definition that for our purposes is very near if not completely correct.

Definition 10.1.1 *A name is a label that (i) singles out a PARTICULAR object and (ii) says NOTHING about the object's properties.*

Part *(ii)* of Def 10.1.1 is not entirely correct. There are certain properties that a name will imply the object it names has. These are properties an object must have before you can do any logic on it. An obvious property is that of having a name. If I name an object, then that object has the property of having a name. Excepting properties like this (properties that an object has to have before you can do logic on it) a name should not imply that the object has any particular properties. The big problem is working out just which properties are the necessary ones. e logic is that the named object exists.

Definition 10.1.2 *In classical logic (predicate logic) if an object is named then it exists. If I name Joey the Martian, then I have also said that Joey the Martian exists. If an object does not exist then I should not name it.*[2]

Definition 10.1.3 *In any sentence that uses names, a predicate is what is left after some or all of the names have been removed.*

When we use names in natural language we occasionally use a name that does suggest some properties of the person who has it. For example the a names like "Peter" and "Jane" certainly have connotations as to the gender of their bearers. However such properties are suggested but never entailed (unless they are trivial properties). In the logical sense a name should not imply anything; if a name implies some property about an object use a different name. In the logic, the name of an object/person does not have to be the same as what the person is called.

Here are some possible sentences and we shall see whether we can immediately pick out the names:

1.   Karen is a carpenter.

       The only name here is "Karen."

2.   My next door neighbour is a carpenter.

       Is the phrase "My next door neighbour" a name? The fact that it is termed a phrase should suggest that we are not going to take it as a name. It is not a name because it implies some property about the object being named; the property of course is that the object is my next door neighbour.

---

[2] After all, there is nothing to name.

3.   Someone is a carpenter.

"Someone" is obviously not a name as it does not single out a particular object.

4.   Everything is a carpenter.

"Everything" is also not a name, it is a quantifier and does not single out a specific object.

5.   Grass is green.

There is argument on whether "grass" is a name. Some say that it is not and it should be read: "All grass....." Others say that "grass" is the name of a generic: grass. This book will prefer to read "Grass is green" as short for "All grass is green" where "grass" is not a name. Please ignore any problems.

There is a generic name for phrases like "My next door neighbour" and "The next person to read this chapter." Phrases such as these are called *titles* or more commonly, as Russell called them, *definite descriptions*. It is a great subject of debate in philosophy of religion whether the word "God" is a name or a title.

10.2   Formalisation of sentences

If we have any atomic sentence we can divide up into a name and predicate, we may also put forward a formalisation for it.

- For the predicate we take capital letters from the middle of the alphabet, usually from "F" upwards.

- For the name we take lower case letters from the start of the alphabet, means from "a" up.

Of course as far as the logic is concerned it is utterly arbitrary what symbols you use as long as you do not have one symbol to signify two separate things. Here is a very atomic sentence and its formalisation, of course there has to be a key.

Jack is a student

This will formalize in the following way:

Key
$\overline{F} = \ldots$ is a student
$a = $ Jack

$F a$ ⟋ Jack
⟍ ... is a student

Notice that the predicate symbol comes before the symbol for the name which itself is a name. Any mathematician will notice that this is very similar to the way he might write a function operating on some term. The mathematical origins of predicate logic become apparent.[3] The symbol for the name should not be written as a subscript; it is written like any normal letter.

Here is another sentence:

Eric is wrapping paper

Key $\underline{Fa}$
$\overline{F} = \ldots$ is wrapping paper
$a = $ Eric

Another sentence:

Blind Owl is going up the country

Key $\underline{Fa}$
$\overline{F} = \ldots$ is going up the country
$a = $ Blind Owl

Provided we keep all these sentences away from each other, it does not matter that we formalize them using the same letters.

Not all atomic sentences and hence not all predicates are *unary* (involving one name); there can be *binary*[4], *tertiary*, and higher relations. Here is a binary relation (involves two names):

Paul loves Grace

There are three possible ways of dealing with this.

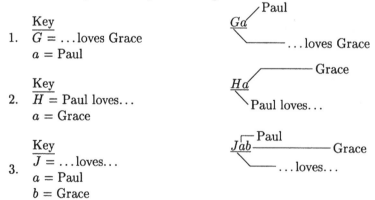

1. Key
    $\overline{G} = \ldots$ loves Grace
    $a = $ Paul

2. Key
    $\overline{H} = $ Paul loves$\ldots$
    $a = $ Grace

3. Key
    $\overline{J} = \ldots$ loves$\ldots$
    $a = $ Paul
    $b = $ Grace

---

[3]Remember that the symbolic notation is for convenience. We could do all the logical work with no formal notation but it would involve much more writing. Further, observing and defining rules or patterns would be more difficult. Some do not bother to formalize names, writing the sentence above $F(jack)$, which looks like a Norwegian swear word is a lot more cumbersome to write. So we will replace Jack and write Fa.

[4]A binary predicate, like "$\ldots$ loves $\ldots$," is sometimes called a *two-place relation*.

None of these three possibilities is incorrect, and not one is always better than the others. However, as a general rule it is better to divide a sentence into as many names and predicates as you can for the same reasons as those for propositional logic (see page 39). Certainly when determining validity in arguments, you will be much better off splitting things up as much as possible.

Predicate logic combines this analysis of basic sentences with the truth functional analysis of propositional logic. With complex sentences you can split them up into truth functions as well as names and predicates. Consider the following sentence:

Gee! Barry is a bee

First, the "Gee!" is an expression of surprise and really carries no meaning in our logic so there is no need to translate it. It would be a little dangerous to analyze the sentence as just a name and a predicate, we can bring in the negation truth function:

Key $\sim Fa$
$F = \ldots$ is a bee
$a = $ Barry

The sentence "$\sim Fa$" reads: "It is not the case that Barry is staying alive." There is another way of analysing this sentence which we shall disallow in this book.

Key $\sim Gab$
$G = \ldots$ is $\ldots$
$a = $ Barry
$b = $ a bee

The problem with this formalisation should be obvious: the phrase "a bee" is not a name here and therefore should not be treated like one. Here is another more complicated sentence:

Paul and Grace like airplanes and starships

There are many ways of formalising this sentence here is one way:

Key Fab
$F = \ldots$ and$\ldots$ like airplanes and
starships
$a = $ Paul
$b = $ Grace

The fact that the a and the b appear after the F tells you what order to put them back into the "$\ldots$ and$\ldots$ like airplanes and starships" when reading the formalized version of the sentence. This formalisation, although not incorrect, can be improved upon from a practical point of view.

Key $Fa \cdot Fb \cdot Ga \cdot Gb$

$G = \ldots$ likes airplanes

$H = \ldots$ likes starships   Paul likes airplanes, Grace likes airplanes,

$a = $ Paul   Paul likes starships   Grace likes starships

$b = $ Grace

This formalisation involves more truth functions, names and predicates and therefore is preferred. We do not count the words "airplanes" and "starships" as names. Here is another sentence:

If Janis does a record she'll get the pearl

We formalize this sentence like this:

Key $Fa \supset Ga$

$F = \ldots$ does a record

$G = \ldots$ will get the pearl

$a = $ Janis

Even though "the pearl" singles out a specific object it is not a name (some predicate is implied about the object namely the predicate "...is a pearl") and so it is not a good idea to treat it like one.[5]

10.3   Exercises

Translate into predicate logic the following sentences so that in each case at least one truth function is represented. You must state which name letter represents which name and which predicate letter represents which predicate. (Name letters should be chosen from $a, b, c \ldots$; predicate letters should be chosen from $F, G, H, \ldots$)

1. Peter will go to the cinema, but Jane will go to the party.

2. If Peter goes to the cinema and uses deodorant, Jane will go too.

3. If Peter does not go to the flat, Jane will not leave him.

4. Peter admires Jane, but Jane does not admire Peter.

5. Peter admires either Mary or Jane.

6. John admires Mary in addition to himself.

7. Shelly will go to the theatre only if Mark goes and Spencer does not go.

---

[5]The following formalisation, for our purposes, is out.

Key $Fa \supset Gab$

$F = \ldots$ does a record

$G = \ldots$ will get $\ldots$

$a = $ Janis

$b = $ The pearl

8. If Jane admires John, she will go to the party with him.

9. York lies between London and Newcastle, but Edinburgh does not.

10. If Mary and John are the parents of Jane, then she respects both of them.

10.4 Quantifiers and Variables

We have not yet said much about quantifiers like "something" or "everything" except that they are definitely not names. It is not so easy to come up with easy examples using those quantifiers so we shall use "everyone" and "someone" instead. Consider the following sentences:

1. Somebody smokes.

2. Everybody smokes.

3. Nobody smokes.

In each one, it is quite easy to spot the predicate: it is "...smokes," however it is not so obvious what to do for the quantifiers used in each sentence. Let us look at the truth conditions for each sentence.

1. "Someone smokes" is true it when there is at least one name (nameing implies existence) which makes the sentence "...smokes" true when the blank is filled in by that name.

2. "Everyone smokes" is true when no matter what name we put in the blank of the predicate "...smokes," the sentence comes out as true.

3. "Nobody smokes" is true when there is no name that we can put in the blank of "...smokes" to make a true sentence. Or when every name we put in the blank of "...smokes," makes the sentence false.

This is not strictly true since names do not just apply to humans; any object whatsoever (as long as it exists) can be named. For the above quantifiers, we have to restrict our naming to humans. Also we are making the major assumption that everything has been named.[6] Here are some quantifiers and predicates which will range over all possible names (and hence all existing things):

1. Something is made up of photons.

2. Everything is made up of photons.

3. Nothing is made up of photons.

---

[6]There are understandings of the quantifiers that do not require this major assumption; they perfectly are intuitive and make little difference to the logic we are doing here.

The predicates from which you have to choose when your quantifiers range over everything are very restricted and not very pleasant.

Have another look at the truth conditions given above. As a matter of fact what we say in the truth conditions is exactly what we say in the logic – we simply formalize it. In the notation we use *quantifiers* and *variables*:

For variables we pick lower case letters from the end of the alphabet, almost always from x up. In the unlikely event that more than three variables are needed you usually hop down to u or v and start up. Here is how to formalize the sentences above about smoking:

Definition 10.4.1

Someone smokes	$(Ex)Fx$
Everyone smokes	$(x)Fx$
$F = \ldots smokes$	

These two formalized sentences read into familiar Loglish:[7]

Definition 10.4.2

Someone smokes	*There is an x such that Fx*
Everyone smokes	*For all x, Fx*
$F = \ldots smokes$	

Where the F stands for "... smokes."

As is common with logic the notation is not universal, there are very similar yet different notations to note.

Quantifier	My notation	The other notation
Existential Quantifier	(Ex)	$(\exists x)$
Universal Quantifier	(x)	$(\forall x)$

Admittedly the other notation is more common, but it frequently is interpreted in a different way.

There is no symbol for the quantifier "nothing," not only that, but there is no name for it either. This is because it is expressible in terms of the other two quantifiers (see truth condition 3 for "nothing", page 157.

Here are some more sentences:

Everybody likes the Zarathustra

$$\dfrac{\text{Key}}{F = \ldots \text{likes the Zarathustra}} \qquad\qquad (x)Fx$$

Because the variable – the x – refers to no object in particular we do not need to put it in the key. Even if the quantifier were an existential one, we could not put the x in the key.

---

[7]Loglish is a language often used in philosophy that is a mish-mash of English and logical terminology. Sometimes it is extremely useful, other times it merely confuses.

Nobody likes to spell Zarathustra

Remember that the truth conditions for "nobody" offers two options. "Nobody smokes" could mean either that everybody does not smoke or that there does not exist a person who does smoke. The two are equivalent; we can express them both.

Key

G=... likes to spell Zarathustra

$(x) \sim Gx$ ——————— likes to spell...

does not / Everybody

Here is the other way:

Key

G=... likes to spell Zarathustra

$\sim(Ex)Gx$ ——————— likes to spell...

There is not / someone who

What about this rather obviously true sentence:

If everyone is boozing then Yoshi is boozing

The sentence formalizes like this:[8]

Key

$F = $ ... is boozing

$a = $ Yoshi

$(x)Fx \supset Fa$

Definition 10.4.3 *The* scope *of a particular quantifier is everything in the brackets immediately to the right. With regard to its scope, a quantifier is similar to negation.*

In the following sentence the scope of the quantifier (x) is underlined:

$$(y)[(x)\underline{(Ez)(Fx \cdot Fz)} \supset Gy]^9$$

The $\supset$ (onwards) is outside the brackets to the right of the (x) and so is outside the scope of the (x).

Now the scope of the quantifier (y) is underlined.

$$(y)\underline{[(x)(Ez)(Fx \cdot Fz) \supset Gy]}$$

And the scope of the quantifier (z).

$$(y)[(x)(Ez)\underline{(Fx \cdot Fz)} \supset Gy]$$

Notice that the quantifier (Ez) has Fx within its scope even though the variable letter is different.

---

[8]If the sentence had been "If everyone is boozing then I am boozing" then formalisation would have been awkward for "I" is not obviously a name. One method is to replace all such pronouns with the names of their referents, this problem is ignored here.

[9]$(x)(Ez)(\ldots)$ is short for $(x)[(Ez)(\ldots)]$.

Definition 10.4.4 *A quantifer binds a variable when the variable is within the scope of the quantifier and the variable letter is the same letter as the one that appears in the quantifier.*

Definition 10.4.5 *A variable is free when it not bound by any quantifier. That is to say that a particular variable is free when it is not within the scope of a quantifier that uses the same letter as the one variable does.*

In this book we shall not allow free variables, every variable should be *bound* by a quantifier. A variable that is not bound by a quantifier is called a *free variable* or sometimes a *floating variable*:[10]

$$(Ex)Fx \cdot G\underline{x} \longleftarrow \text{This is a free variable}$$

However in this sentence:

$$(Ex)(Fx \cdot Gx)$$

there are no free variables, and it says that there is an object which has predicate F and predicate G.

$$(x)Fx \supset (Ey)(Fy \cdot \underline{Gx}) \longleftarrow \text{This is a free variable}$$

This variable, even though it is directly after a quantifier, is still free because the quantifier uses a different letter.

$$(x)Fx \cdot Fa$$

There are no free variables in this sentence. Remember that a letter from the beginning of the alphabet should be taken as a name; a name is not a variable and does not need a quantifier to go with it.

Consider the following sentence:

Annie smokes and drinks

We can formalize this sentence:

Key
$\overline{F = \ldots \text{smokes}}$
$G = \ldots \text{drinks}$
$a = \text{Annie}$

$\underbrace{Fa \cdot Ga}$ — and — Annie drinks
$\searrow$ Annie smokes

This is a correct formalisation of the sentence. However, consider this:

Someone smokes and drinks

---

[10]It is not the case that free variables have no meaning; they most certainly do and can be very useful. However, for the purposes of this book, they are not needed and so shall be ignored.

We cannot formalize it in the way we did with "Annie smokes and drinks." Look at what happens if we do:

Key	$(Ex)Fx \cdot (Ex)Gx$
$F = \ldots$ smokes	
$G = \ldots$ drinks	

The formalisation we have put forward above reads as "someone smokes and someone drinks." Note that the smoker and the drinker need not be the same person, for there is a separate quantifier for each predicate (it does not matter that the variable letters of the quantifiers are the same). However, in the original sentence "someone smokes and drinks," the smoker and drinker are the same. This suggests that the two sentences "someone smokes and drinks" and "someone smokes and someone drinks" are different. Look at them again:

1. Someone smokes and drinks.

2. Someone smokes and someone drinks.

The two are clearly different. Here is how the first sentence should be formalized:

Key	$(Ex)(Fx \cdot Gx)$
$F = \ldots$ smokes	
$G = \ldots$ drinks	

The crucial point is that Fx and Gx are bound by the same quantifier.

1. $(Ex)(Fx \cdot Gx)$ is only true when there is (at least) one person who both smokes and drinks.

2. $(Ex)Fx \cdot (Ex)Gx$ is true when at least one person smokes and at least one person drinks. This sentence is true if sentence (1) is true. However sentence (2) can be true without sentence (1) being true.

Here is another example:

Annie is either speeding or shovelling snow

This formalizes quite easily:

Key	$Fa \vee Ga$
$F = \ldots$ is speeding	
$G = \ldots$ is shovelling snow	
$a = $ Annie	

But picture this:

Everyone is either speeding or shovelling snow

We cannot formalize this sentence like we did with the sentence about Annie. See what happens if we do:

Key
$F = \ldots$ is speeding
$G = \ldots$ is shovelling snow

$$(x)Fx \vee (x)Gx$$

Either everyone is F
or everyone is G

The sentence $(x)Fx \vee (x)Gx$ means that either everyone is speeding or everyone is shovelling snow. That is not right; we want it so that any person is either speeding or shovelling. Here is how to write it properly:

Key
$F = \ldots$ is speeding
$G = \ldots$ is shovelling snow

$$(x)(Fx \vee Gx)$$

Everyone
is either an F or a G

As a general rule (although there are exceptions), it is a good idea to have exactly as many quantifiers in the formalisation of a sentence as there are in the original English.

10.4.1   An important and helpful convention

Since confusion may arise when there are many quantifiers in a sentence, we shall introduce a convention. *The convention makes no logical difference, and it is mostly no disaster to break it* but it is helpful to keep.

Definition 10.4.6 (Variable convention) *In any sentence no two quantifiers may use the same variable letter.*

As long as there are enough variables to use, the convention is easy to follow. Find the two examples in this section which breach the variable convention.

10.5   Sentences with multiple Quantifiers

Of course it is possible to have a sentence that uses more than one quantifier in many different places. When you have multiple quantifiers as opposed to multiple names, formalisation becomes tricky. Consider the following two sentences:

1. Ike loves Tina

2. Tina is loved by Ike

The two sentences have identical truth conditions: if Ike loves Tina, then Tina is loved by Ike. However, consider this pair of sentences using the same predicates:

1. Everybody loves somebody

2. Somebody is loved by everybody

These two sentences appear to have different truth conditions. True, if somebody is loved by everybody then everybody loves somebody. However if everybody loves somebody then it does not follow that there is a person that everybody loves. Think of it diagrammatically:

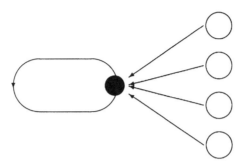

Someone is loved by everyone

The circles represent people, and the arrows represent them loving each other; the filled circle is the person that everybody loves. In this diagram everyone loves someone, and all the circles have a line leading to another circle (in one case it is the same, a narcissist). However, here is another diagram that represents, "Everybody loves somebody":

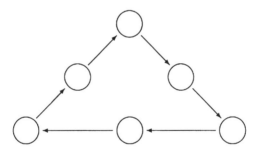

Everyone loves someone

In this love triangle it is clear that everyone loves someone, however it is false that somebody is loved by everybody.[11]

The question remains how to split up sentences with multiple quantifiers. Here are four sentences that are all very different:

1. Everybody loves somebody

2. Somebody is loved by everybody

3. Somebody loves everybody

---

[11] Admittedly the two sentences are ambiguous (and famously so), each can have the natural reading of the other in special conditions.

4. Everybody is loved by somebody

Each of these sentences contains differences from the others. For example (3) and (4) entail that everyone gets loved whereas (1) and (2) do not, although they do entail that everybody does some loving, a whole lot'a'loving.

To determine how to formalize these sentences, we must look at their truth conditions. Take the sentence "Somebody loves everybody."

- The predicate is rather obvious. Let us formalize it with L. So we get Lab meaning a loves b.

- When is the sentence "Somebody loves everybody" true? We shall divide the sentence as follows:

Somebody‖   loves everybody

Thus the sentence "Somebody loves everybody" is true if AT LEAST ONE of these sentences is true:

$(x)Lax$ ⎯⎯ For all x ⎯⎯ a loves x
$(x)Lbx$
$(x)Lcx$
⋮   ⋮

The point is that "Somebody loves everybody" is true when there is a name that we can substitute in this gap; $(x)L\_x$ or when there is a name (person) that correctly fills "...loves everybody."

- But (under our major assumptions) to say there is a name is to say there is an object which is the existential quantifier.[12] We formalize "Somebody loves everybody" like this:

Key
$L = \ldots$ loves $\ldots$

$(Ey)(x)Lyx$ ⎯⎯ There is a y s.t[13] ⎯⎯ y loves x
⎯⎯ for all x

The variables (x and y) MUST be different (see Def 10.4.6). Here is an idea of what would happen otherwise:

1. $(Ex)(x)Lxx$ reads that there is an object such that everybody loves themselves; it is a verbose way of saying everybody loves themselves (the short way is $(x)Lxx$).

2. $(Ey)(x)Lxx$ is logically equivalent to the sentence in (1).

---

[12] We are assuming that every existing object is named, and all names represent existing objects.

[13] "s.t" abbreviates "such that."

We could always have written it like this:

Key
$L = \ldots$ loves $\ldots$

$$(E\overset{\displaystyle\ulcorner\text{There is a } x \text{ s.t}}{x})(y)Lxy \underset{\underset{\displaystyle\text{for all } y}{\textstyle\diagdown\rule{1cm}{0.4pt}}}{\overset{\displaystyle\rule{1cm}{0.4pt}\ x \text{ loves } y}{}}$$

The particular variables chosen are not important; the order of the different variables is the important thing.

What about the sentence in the passive: "Everybody is loved by somebody."

- The predicate is clearly "...is loved by..."; let us formalize it by the letter H.

- Once again we choose to split the sentence at the first quantifier:

  Everybody‖   is loved by somebody.

- The sentence is true when ALL of the following sentences are true:

$$(E\overset{\displaystyle\ulcorner\rule{1cm}{0.4pt}\text{There is an } x \text{ s.t}}{x})Hax \overset{\displaystyle\rule{2cm}{0.4pt}\ a \text{ is loved by } x}{}$$
$$(Ex)Hbx$$
$$(Ex)Hcx$$
$$\vdots \quad \vdots$$

But we can rewrite all these sentences in terms of the predicate L (...loves... by switching round the letters:

$$(E\overset{\displaystyle\ulcorner\rule{1cm}{0.4pt}\text{There is an } x \text{ s.t}}{x})Lxa \overset{\displaystyle\rule{1.5cm}{0.4pt}\ x \text{ loves } a}{}$$
$$(Ex)Lxb$$
$$(Ex)Lxc$$
$$\vdots \quad \vdots$$

What these say is that there is someone that loves a, there is someone who loves b, there is someone who loves c, etc. This goes on for any name.

- So "Everybody is loved by somebody" is true when you can fill any name into the blank space in this sentence: $(Ex)Lx\_$.

- Now formalize the last bullet. Here is what it comes to:

Key
$L = \ldots$ loves $\ldots$

$$(y)\overset{\displaystyle\ulcorner\text{For every } y}{(}Ex)Lxy \underset{\underset{\displaystyle\text{there is an } x \text{ s.t}}{\textstyle\diagdown\rule{1cm}{0.4pt}}}{\overset{\displaystyle\rule{1cm}{0.4pt}\ x \text{ loves } y}{}}$$

Again, the variable letters (x and y) MUST be different. Naturally we could also write it like this:

Key
$L = \ldots$ loves $\ldots$

$$(x)\overset{\displaystyle\ulcorner\text{For every } x}{(}Ey)Lyx \underset{\underset{\displaystyle\text{there is an } y \text{ s.t}}{\textstyle\diagdown\rule{1cm}{0.4pt}}}{\overset{\displaystyle\rule{1cm}{0.4pt}\ y \text{ loves } x}{}}$$

Here is a general procedure for how to formalize a sentence like "Somebody is loved by everybody."

1. Write the quantifiers in the same order as they appear in the sentence. So for "Somebody is loved by everybody" the quantifiers will go like this: $(Ex)(y)\ldots$.

2. Use always the active predicate. Here that means use the predicate "$\ldots$loves$\ldots$," let us use L.

3. If the predicate in the original sentence is in the active write the variables in the same order as the quantifiers. So with the sentence "Somebody loves everybody" we write the following: $(Ex)(y)Lxy$.

4. If the predicate in the original sentence is in the passive (e.g. $\ldots$ is loved by$\ldots$), write the variable letters in reverse order to the way they appear in the quantifiers. So for "Somebody is loved by everybody" we write: $(Ex)(y)Lyx$.

Here is how the four combinations of sentence translate:

Definition 10.5.1

Natural language	Formalization
Everybody loves somebody	$(x)(Ey)Lxy$
Everybody is loved by somebody	$(x)(Ey)Lyx$
Somebody loves everybody	$(Ex)(y)Lxy$
Somebody is loved by everybody	$(Ex)(y)Lyx$

Here is how the formalisations translate back into Loglish:

Formalization	How the formalization reads
$(x)(Ey)Lxy$	For every x, there is a y such that x loves y
$(x)(Ey)Lyx$	For every x, there is a y such that y loves x
$(Ex)(y)Lxy$	There is an x such that for all y, x loves y
$(Ex)(y)Lyx$	There is an x such that for all y, y loves x

10.6   Syllogisms in predicate logic

Finally, we shall deal with the form of sentence you would find in a syllogism, a surprisingly useful aid to developing an understanding of predicate logic. There are of course four types of sentence to play with.

1. **A** form sentences: All A are B.

2. **E** form sentences: No A is B.

3. **I** form sentences: Some A are B.

4. **O** form sentences: Some A are not B.

Remember that the **I** and **O** form sentences use the word "some" to mean there exists at least one. The **I** and **O** forms are not difficult to formalize. Let us look at their truth conditions:

1. An **I** form sentence: for example

   Some students do lots of work.[14]

   This is true when there exists at least one object that is a student AND does lots of work. We can write this down:

   Key
   $F = \ldots$ is a student
   $G = \ldots$ does lots of work

   $$\underset{\text{student}}{\overset{\text{There is a}}{(Ex)(Fx \cdot Gx)}}\text{—}\overset{\text{who does}}{\underset{\text{lots of work.}}{}}$$

2. An **O** form sentence:

   Some students do not do lots of work.

   This is true when there is at least one object that is a student AND does not do lots of work. We can write this down:

   Key
   $F = \ldots$ is a student
   $G = \ldots$ does lots of work

   $$\underset{\text{student}}{\overset{\text{There is a}}{(Ex)(Fx \cdot \sim Gx)}}\text{—}\overset{\text{who does not do}}{\underset{\text{lots of work.}}{}}$$

3. An **A** form sentence:

   All students do lots of work.

   This is true when there does not exist something that is both a student and does not do lots of work:

   Key $\sim(Ex)(Fx \cdot \sim Gx)$
   $F = \ldots$ is a student
   $G = \ldots$ does lots of work

4. An **E** form sentence:

   No student does lots of work.

   This is true when there does not exist something that is both a student and does lots of work:

   Key $\sim(Ex)(Fx \cdot Gx)$
   $F = \ldots$ is a student
   $G = \ldots$ does lots of work

---

[14]Or: Some student does lots of work.

Have a look at these four sentences again, arranged in the format of the square of opposition:

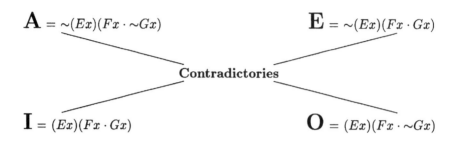

$$\mathbf{A} = \sim(Ex)(Fx \cdot \sim Gx)$$

$$\mathbf{E} = \sim(Ex)(Fx \cdot Gx)$$

Contradictories

$$\mathbf{I} = (Ex)(Fx \cdot Gx)$$

$$\mathbf{O} = (Ex)(Fx \cdot \sim Gx)$$

The only aspect of Aristotle's logic that is maintained is the contradiction rule. The **A** and the **O** contradict each other (one is the negation of the other), and so do the **E** and the **I**.

There is another way of doing a universal sentence (the **A** and the **E**). Consider the sentence "All boors will be horribly maimed." The sentence is true when for any object (person), if it is boorish then it will be horribly maimed. This gives us the following formalisation:

|For every x
Key
$F = \ldots$ is a boor $(x)(Fx \supset Gx)$——— then x will be horribly maimed.
$G = \ldots$ will be horribly maimed |if x is a boor

The rather shocking sentence "No boor will be horribly maimed" can also be formalized in this fashion:

|For every x
Key
$F = \ldots$ is a boor $(x)(Fx \supset \sim Gx)$——— then x will not be horribly maimed.
$G = \ldots$ will be horribly maimed |if x is a boor

From this we can derive an important result. Any one of the two quantifiers can express the other quantifier.

1. A sentence like $(x)(\ldots)$ has the same truth conditions as $\sim(Ex) \sim (\ldots)$.

2. A sentence like $(Ex)(\ldots)$ has the same truth conditions as $\sim(x) \sim (\ldots)$.

As a matter of fact Bertrand Russell, one of the world's great philosophers and mathematical logicians, sought to abolish the existential quantifier completely and use nothing but the universal quantifier. His logic books soon became bulky and very inefficient.[15]

---

[15]See *Principia Mathematica*, Bertrand Russell and Alfred North Whitehead (1910, 1912, 1913).

10.7 Buckets of eggs

Here are some examples of sentences and their formalisations. The bracketing is relaxed a little.

All cats are furry

Key

$C = \dots$ is a cat

$F = \dots$ is furry

$$(x)(Cx \supset Fx)$$

Adam has an ant

Key

$H = \dots$ has $\dots$

$C = \dots$ is an ant

$a = $ Adam

$$(Ex)(Hax \cdot Cx)$$

No philosopher is a waste of space

Key

$P = \dots$ is a philosopher

$W = \dots$ is a waste of space

$$(x)(Px \supset {\sim}Wx)^{16}$$

There is a banana that is long and straight

Key

$S = \dots$ is a banana

$L = \dots$ is long

$S = \dots$ is straight

$$(Ex)(Bx \cdot Lx \cdot Sx)$$

All T. S. Eliot's poetry is depressing and sad

Key

$a = $ T. S. Eliot

$F = \dots$ is poetry

$B = \dots$ is by$\dots$

$G = \dots$ is depressing

$H = \dots$ is sad

$$(x)[(Fx \cdot Bxa) \supset (Gx \cdot Hx)]$$

Someone controls everything

Key

$H = \dots$ is a person

$F = \dots$ controls$\dots$

$$(Ex)(y)(Hx \cdot Fxy)^{17}$$

---

[16] Or ${\sim}(Ex)(Px \cdot Wx)$.

[17] Or $(Ex)(Hx \cdot (y)Fxy)$

Everything is controlled by someone

Key $(x)(Ey)(Hy \cdot Fyx)$
$H = \ldots$ is a person
$F = \ldots$ controls...

The predicate "... is a person" is necessary to distinguish between the different randges of the two quantifiers "someone" and "everything."

It is only the students who overwork who are the robots

Key $(x)(Fx \supset (Tx \supset Sx))^{18}$
$F = \ldots$ is a student
$S = \ldots$ overworks
$T = \ldots$ is a robot

Food and drink were consumed at the party

Key $(Ex)(Fx \cdot Px) \cdot (Ey)(Dy \cdot Py)$
$F = \ldots$ is food
$D = \ldots$ is drink
$P = \ldots$ was consumed at the party

All bald men hate themselves

Key $(x)[(Bx \cdot Mx) \supset Hxx]$
$B = \ldots$ is bald
$M = \ldots$ is a man
$H = \ldots$ hates...

Every bald man hates a man with hair

Key $(x)[(Mx \cdot Bx) \supset (y)[(My \cdot \sim By) \supset Hxy]]^{19}$
$B = \ldots$ is bald
$M = \ldots$ is a man
$H = \ldots$ hates...

"Every bald man hates a man with hair" is an ambiguous sentence. There are at least three ways to read it:

1. Every bald man hates all non-bald men. This is the way we have formalized it above.

2. Every bald man has singled out at least one non-bald man and hates him.

---

[18] Or $(x)(Fx \supset (Tx \equiv Sx))$ if you think the "It is only" means "only and all" but this MUST be stated.

[19] $(x)(y)[(Mx \cdot Bx \cdot My \cdot \sim By)] \supset Hxy]$ is simpler, but has little of the orginal structure of the English.

3. All bald men hate this one man who is also non-bald.

(3) is quite easy to formalize:

Every bald man hates a man with hair

Key $\qquad\qquad\qquad (Ey)[My \cdot \sim By \cdot (x)((Mx \cdot Bx) \supset Hxy)]$

$B = \ldots$ is bald
$M = \ldots$ is a man
$H = \ldots$ hates...

Here is how to formalize the reading given by (2).

Every bald man hates a man with hair

Key $\qquad\qquad\qquad (x)[(Mx \cdot Bx) \supset (Ey)(My \cdot \sim By \cdot Hxy)]$

$B = \ldots$ is bald
$M = \ldots$ is a man
$H = \ldots$ hates...

Every bald man hates a man with hair whom he sees

Key $\qquad\qquad (x)(y)[(Mx \cdot Bx \cdot My \cdot \sim By \cdot Hxy \cdot Sxy) \supset Hxy]$

$B = \ldots$ is bald
$M = \ldots$ is a man
$H = \ldots$ hates...
$S = \ldots$ sees...

Peter does nothing and Jane does something

Key $\qquad\qquad\qquad \sim Fa \cdot Fb$

$a =$ Peter
$b =$ Jane
$F = \ldots$ does something

The problem with the last example is that we do not know exactly what "nothing" and "something" mean in this context. All we know for sure is that if you do not "do nothing" then you "do something." It is possible to twist and turn with the quantifiers and bring in all sorts of weird predicates but it is much simpler just to use the predicate "...does something.'

If Peter does not exist, then he both is and is not Elvis.

Existence is not a predicate in the system of this book; every name has a bearer.[20]

Finally I shall show how to analyze some arguments not analysable in propositional logic or using the form of Venn diagram we were using earlier. The first is easy:

---

[20]Though there are systems where existence is a predicate and there are non-referring names, or even non-existent objects.

Anyone studying over the summer is mad
Anna studies during the summer
_____
Anna is mad

$(x)(Sx \supset Mx)$
$\underline{Sa}$
Ma

It should be obvious what all the letters mean.

All cats are mammals
_____
All cats' heads are mammals' heads

The first line is easy. We shall do the second line in steps:

1. All cats heads are mammals heads

2. $(x)(x$ is a head of a cat $\supset x$ is a head of a mammal$)$

3. $(x)[(Ey)(y$ is a cat$\cdot x$ is a head of$y)\supset(Ez)(z$ is a mammal$\cdot x$ is a head of$z)]$

4. $(x)[\ (Ey)(Fy \cdot Hxy) \supset (Ez)(Gz \cdot Hxz)\ ]$

So the argument is formalized as:

$(x)(Fx \supset Gx)$
_____
$(x)[\ (Ey)(Fy \cdot Hxy) \supset (Ez)(Gz \cdot Hxz)\ ]$

Key
_____
$F = \ldots$ is a cat
$G = \ldots$ is a mammal
$H = \ldots$ is a head of...

In the next chapter, we shall show how to prove these arguments to be valid.

10.8   Exercises

Translate the following sentences into predicate logic so that every name is represented by a name letter (the same name letter for the same name) and every quantifier expression is replaced by a quantifier. State explicitly which name letter represents which name and which predicate letter represents which predicate.

1. Someone is happy.

2. Everybody breathes.

3. No-one is a logician.

4. Everybody hates Jane.

5. John likes somebody.

6. John likes some dog

7. Someone likes some dog

8. Some cat likes some dog

9. Every cat likes some dog

10. Some dog is liked by every cat

11. Every student likes Jane.

12. Some students dislike John.

13. John likes nobody.

14. Everyone is someone's child.

15. Somebody created everybody.

16. Someone will go to the theatre but everybody will go to the party.

17. If a farmer has a chicken, he plucks it.

18. If Peter goes to the cinema everyone will go too.

19. If Peter does not go to the cinema no-one will go.

20. Jane likes everyone but not everyone likes Jane.

21. Every student likes logic.

22. Everybody likes themselves.

23. Every politician admires themselves.

24. Everyone pleases someone in addition to themselves.

25. Peter will get drunk only if everyone does.

26. Everyone marries either a person or a job.

Chapter 11

Tableaux And Identity

11.1 A BIG warning

Predicate logic has an annoying and interesting property. In a tableau for propositional logic you need use each line only once (the tick is there to let you know you have used it). In predicate logic you can use each line of the tableau as many times as you like. The tick lets you know that you have used a sentence so you can use all the sentences once before using any of them again. Because you can use a sentence more than once, if you do not hit a contradiction by the time you have used each line, you cannot conclude that the sentence you are analysing is not logically necessary (see Section 11.9).

11.2 The extra rules

We have shown how to turn a sentence in natural language into predicate logic, and how many sentences in English can be analyzed by it. What is now needed is a deduction system to go with it. We shall use an advanced form of the deduction system for propositional logic, the only difference being a few extra rules.

Let us first see if some sentences in predicate logic are logically necessary (there is no way for them to be false under our logical principles) or not:

$$(x)Fx \supset Fa$$

This sentence states the rather obvious proposition that, if all objects have property F then the object a has property F. The way it is proved is by a simple tableau. First we assume the sentence is false:

$$\textbf{F} \quad (x)Fx \supset Fa$$

Since the main connective is a material implication that has an F (false) at the side, we bring down the antecedent as true and the consequent as false:

$$\mathbf{F} \quad (x)Fx \supset Fa \; \checkmark$$
$$\mathbf{T} \quad (x)Fx$$
$$\mathbf{F} \quad Fa$$

A new rule

Now we introduce a new rule for predicate logic, which says that if you have a sentence with a universal quantifier as the main connective – a sentence that looks like $(x)(\ldots)$ and has a T by it – you can bring it down and substitute any letter you like for the variable (the x).

If we see this line in a tableau:

$$\mathbf{T} \quad (x)(\; \sim(Fx \supset (Ey)(Gx \cdot Hy))\;)$$

we can bring it down like this:

$$\mathbf{T} \quad \sim(Fa \supset (Ey)(Ga \cdot Hy))$$

We could also have brought it down like this if we wanted:

$$\mathbf{T} \quad \sim(Fb \supset (Ey)(Gb \cdot Hy))$$

Note that it is only the variable x that is substituted out; we can deal with only one variable per line.

We can apply this rule to the tableaux we were doing. If we can pick a letter that causes a contradiction then we should use it:

$$\mathbf{F} \quad (x)Fx \supset Fa \; \checkmark$$
$$\mathbf{T} \quad (x)Fx \; \checkmark$$
$$\mathbf{F} \quad Fa$$
$$\mathbf{T} \quad Fa$$
$$\times$$

We brought down the $(x)Fx$ as Fa and thence generated a contradiction. The sentence $(x)Fx \supset Fa$ is a logical necessity. Here is a slightly more complicated sentence:

$$(x)Fx \supset (Ey)Fy$$

This sentence says that if all objects have property F then there exists an object that has property F. In order to check whether this sentence is a logical necessity, we have to assume it is false.

$$\mathbf{F} \quad (x)Fx \supset (Ey)Fy$$

Since we have a false material implication, we can bring it down without branching:

$$\begin{array}{ll} \textbf{F} & (x)Fx \supset (Ey)Fy \ \surd \\ \textbf{T} & (x)Fx \\ \textbf{F} & (Ey)Fy \end{array}$$

A new rule

As with a true universal (**T** $(x)(\ldots)$) when we bring down a line like this:

$$\textbf{F} \quad (Ex)Fx$$

we can substitute any name we like for the x to get this line.

$$\textbf{F} \quad Fa$$

In the original example it makes no difference which line we bring down first as both cover all letters (with a true (x) you can substitute any letter you like for the x, the same goes for a false (Ex)). Here is the first:

$$\begin{array}{ll} \textbf{F} & (x)Fx \supset (Ey)Fy \ \surd \\ \textbf{T} & (x)Fx \ \surd \\ \textbf{F} & (Ey)Fy) \\ \textbf{T} & Fa \end{array}$$

And here is the second:

$$\begin{array}{ll} \textbf{F} & (x)Fx \supset (Ey)Fy \ \surd \\ \textbf{T} & (x)Fx \ \surd \\ \textbf{F} & (Ey)Fy \\ \textbf{T} & Fa \\ \textbf{F} & Fa \\ & \times \end{array}$$

When substituting a variable for a letter – e.g. going from $(Ex)(Fx \cdot Gx)$ to $Fa \cdot Ga$) – you should always keep the truth value. So if $(Ex)(Fx \cdot Gx)$ has a T beside it in the tableau then so should the $Fa \cdot Ga$.

What the last logical necessity shows us is that in Classical logic something must exist; it cannot apply to situations in which nothing exists. There are a number of ways of dealing with this, if it is thought of as a problem; for example, creatures called *Free logics* are designed to handle non-existence.

Here is another more complicated sentence:

$$(x)Fx \supset \sim(Ey)(\sim Fy)$$

This sentence reads in Loglish as "If all x are F then it is not the case that there is an x which is not F," which translates as "If everything is F then there is nothing which is not F." This is not a very elusive statement; it should be intuitive that it is a logical necessity. To prove it we first assume that it is false:

$$\mathbf{F} \quad (x)Fx \supset \sim(Ey)(\sim Fy)$$

The main connective is a material implication so we bring it down just as we would in propositional logic:

$$
\begin{array}{ll}
\mathbf{F} & (x)Fx \supset \sim(Ey)(\sim Fy) \ \checkmark \\
\mathbf{T} & (x)Fx \\
\mathbf{F} & \sim(Ey)(\sim Fy)
\end{array}
$$

We also treat the negation in exactly the same way. When doing a tableau in Predicate Logic you should always get rid of as many truth functions as you can before dealing with the quantifiers. However with a sentence like $(x)(\sim Fx)$, deal with the quantifier first as the truth function is inside the quantifiers brackets.

$$
\begin{array}{ll}
\mathbf{F} & (x)Fx \supset \sim(Ey)(\sim Fy) \ \checkmark \\
\mathbf{T} & (x)Fx \\
\mathbf{F} & \sim(Ey)(\sim Fy) \ \checkmark \\
\mathbf{T} & (Ey)(\sim Fy)
\end{array}
$$

A new rule

We now come to another rule of predicate logic. If you see a sentence bound by an existential quantifier which has a T beside it, you can bring it down, like the universal quantifier, with any letter you like provided that that letter has not occurred above the new line you wish to create (above, that is, in the same branch). Suppose we come across this setup:

$$
\begin{array}{ll}
\mathbf{F} & Fa \\
\mathbf{T} & (Ex)Fx
\end{array}
$$

We cannot bring down the second line using an a; we would have to bring down another letter, e.g. b. In order to get the maximum effect from the deduction system, it is best to do the true existential lines first (unless there is no choice)

In our example we shall bring down the $(Ex)(\sim Fx)$ first.

$$
\begin{array}{ll}
\mathbf{F} & (x)Fx \supset \sim(Ey)(\sim Fy) \ \checkmark \\
\mathbf{T} & (x)Fx \\
\mathbf{F} & \sim(Ey)(\sim Fy) \ \checkmark \\
\mathbf{T} & (Ey)(\sim Fy) \ \checkmark \\
\mathbf{T} & \sim Fa
\end{array}
$$

We can now eliminate the negation:

$$
\begin{array}{ll}
\mathbf{F} & (x)Fx \supset \sim(Ey)(\sim Fy) \ \checkmark \\
\mathbf{T} & (x)Fx \\
\mathbf{F} & \sim(Ey)(\sim Fy) \ \checkmark \\
\mathbf{T} & (Ey)(\sim Fy) \ \checkmark \\
\mathbf{T} & \sim Fa \ \checkmark \\
\mathbf{F} & Fa
\end{array}
$$

We can bring down the $(x)Fx$ useing any letter we like, regardless of what has occurred before. It makes most sense to use an a as that will immediately hit a contradiction:

$$
\begin{array}{ll}
\textbf{F} & (x)Fx \supset \sim(Ey)(\sim Fy) \;\checkmark \\
\textbf{T} & (x)Fx \\
\textbf{F} & \sim(Ey)(\sim Fy) \;\checkmark \\
\textbf{T} & (Ey)(\sim Fy) \;\checkmark \\
\textbf{T} & \sim Fa \;\checkmark \\
\textbf{F} & Fa \\
\textbf{T} & Fa \\
& \times
\end{array}
$$

There is a contradiction: the sentence is a logical necessity.

$$\sim(Ex)(\sim Fx) \supset (y)Fy$$

Let us do the indirect proof:

$$
\begin{array}{ll}
\textbf{F} & \sim(Ex)(\sim Fx) \supset (y)Fy
\end{array}
$$

The false material implication goes :

$$
\begin{array}{ll}
\textbf{F} & \sim(Ex)(\sim Fx) \supset (y)Fy \;\checkmark \\
\textbf{T} & \sim(Ex)(\sim Fx) \\
\textbf{F} & (y)Fy
\end{array}
$$

Next we get rid of the negation. We must always take out the truth functions first:

$$
\begin{array}{ll}
\textbf{F} & \sim(Ex)(\sim Fx) \supset (y)Fy \;\checkmark \\
\textbf{T} & \sim(Ex)(\sim Fx) \;\checkmark \\
\textbf{F} & (y)Fy \\
\textbf{F} & (Ex)(\sim Fx)
\end{array}
$$

A new rule

The next new rule is that when we have a false universal like this:

$$\textbf{F} \quad (x)(\ldots)^{[1]}$$

we treat it in the same way as a true existential line and only substitute for the x a letter that has not been used before in the tableaux.

It is best to bring down false universal quantifiers, or true existential quantifiers first.

---

[1]Or $(y)(\ldots)$ or $(z)(\ldots)$ etc.

$$\begin{array}{ll} \textbf{F} & \sim(Ex)(\sim Fx) \supset (y)Fy \; \checkmark \\ \textbf{T} & \sim(Ex)(\sim Fx) \; \checkmark \\ \textbf{F} & (y)Fy \; \checkmark \\ \textbf{F} & (Ex)(\sim Fx) \\ \textbf{F} & Fa \end{array}$$

Now for the remaining line, remember that a false existential line can use any letter you like. It is always a good idea when bring down a line that allows you to use any letter, to use a letter you have already used before:

$$\begin{array}{ll} \textbf{F} & \sim(Ex)(\sim Fx) \supset (y)Fy \; \checkmark \\ \textbf{T} & \sim(Ex)(\sim Fx) \; \checkmark \\ \textbf{F} & (y)Fy \; \checkmark \\ \textbf{F} & (Ex)(\sim Fx) \; \checkmark \\ \textbf{F} & Fa \\ \textbf{F} & \sim Fa \end{array}$$

And to finish:

$$\begin{array}{ll} \textbf{F} & \sim(Ex)(\sim Fx) \supset (y)Fy \; \checkmark \\ \textbf{T} & \sim(Ex)(\sim Fx) \; \checkmark \\ \textbf{F} & (y)Fy \; \checkmark \\ \textbf{F} & (Ex)(\sim Fx) \; \checkmark \\ \textbf{F} & Fa \\ \textbf{F} & \sim Fa \; \checkmark \\ \textbf{T} & Fa \\ & \times \end{array}$$

The sentence is a logical necessity. If you compare the last two examples, you should will that the material implication is the other way round:

1. $(x)Fx \supset \sim(Ey)(\sim Fy)$

2. $\sim(Ex)(\sim Fx) \supset (y)Fy$

The following sentences also are logical necessities (because the two sentences above take the same truth values):

1. $(x)Fx \equiv \sim(Ex)(\sim Fx)$

2. $\sim(x)Fx \equiv (Ex)(\sim Fx)$

The above two sentences are logically equivalent, if you do not see how this is so go back and look at the propositional logic chapters again.

Here is a list of the new rules we have produced for doing a predicate logic tableau. They are all the extra rules necessary.

Negation

T	$\sim A$
F	A

F	$\sim A$
T	A

Conjunction

T	$A \cdot B$
T	A
T	B

$$F \quad A \cdot B$$
$$\diagup \quad \diagdown$$
$$\text{F } A \quad \text{F } B$$

Disjunction

$$T \quad A \vee B$$
$$\diagup \quad \diagdown$$
$$\text{T } A \quad \text{T } B$$

F	$A \vee B$
F	A
F	B

Material Implication

$$T \quad A \supset B$$
$$\diagup \quad \diagdown$$
$$\text{F } A \quad \text{T } B$$

F	$A \supset B$
T	A
F	B

Universal Quantification

T	$(x)Fx$
T	Fa

F	$(x)Fx$
F	Fa^*

Existential Quantification

T	$(Ex)Fx$
T	Fa^*

F	$(Ex)Fx$
F	Fa

*The name used here must not have been used
anywhere above it in the same branch

$$(Ey)Fy \supset \sim(x) \sim Fx$$

From the last chapter we know that this sentence is a logical necessity: if
someone is F, then it is not the case that everyone is not F.

$$\mathbf{F} \quad (Ey)Fy \supset \sim(z) \sim Fx$$

The main connective is a material implication and we all know what to do with that:

$$\mathbf{F} \quad (Ey)Fy \supset \sim(x) \sim Fx \ \checkmark$$
$$\mathbf{T} \quad ((Ey)Fy$$
$$\mathbf{F} \quad \sim(x) \sim Fx$$

Next we get rid of the remaining truth functions not bounded by quantifiers:

$$\mathbf{F} \quad (Ey)Fy \supset \sim(x) \sim Fx \ \checkmark$$
$$\mathbf{T} \quad (Ey)Fy$$
$$\mathbf{F} \quad \sim(x) \sim Fx \ \checkmark$$
$$\mathbf{T} \quad (x) \sim Fx$$

There are no truth functions outside the quantifiers, so the next step is to bring down a quantifier. You should always bring down first the quantifier that has a restriction on what name you can use. The only quantifier here with a restriction on it is the true existential quantifier:[2]

$$\mathbf{F} \quad (Ey)Fy \supset \sim(x) \sim Fx \ \checkmark$$
$$\mathbf{T} \quad (Ey)Fy \ \checkmark$$
$$\mathbf{F} \quad \sim(x) \sim Fx \ \checkmark$$
$$\mathbf{T} \quad (x) \sim Fx$$
$$\mathbf{T} \quad Fa$$

Now the nextun-ticked line:

$$\mathbf{F} \quad (Ey)Fy \supset \sim(x) \sim Fx \ \checkmark$$
$$\mathbf{T} \quad (Ey)Fy \ \checkmark$$
$$\mathbf{F} \quad \sim(x) \sim Fx \ \checkmark$$
$$\mathbf{T} \quad (x) \sim Fx \ \checkmark$$
$$\mathbf{T} \quad Fa$$
$$\mathbf{T} \quad \sim Fa$$

Finally we bring down the only un-ticked line:

$$\mathbf{F} \quad (Ey)Fy \supset \sim(x) \sim Fx \ \checkmark$$
$$\mathbf{T} \quad (Ey)Fy \ \checkmark$$
$$\mathbf{F} \quad \sim(x) \sim Fx \ \checkmark$$
$$\mathbf{T} \quad (x) \sim Fx \ \checkmark$$
$$\mathbf{T} \quad Fa$$
$$\mathbf{T} \quad \sim Fa \ \checkmark$$
$$\mathbf{F} \quad Fa$$
$$\times$$

---

[2]The universal quantifier has a negation inside it: $\mathbf{T} \ (x) \sim Fx$. As long as the negation is not the main connective we need not concern ourselves with it.

As there is a contradiction the sentence is a logical necessity. Here is the sentence with the material implication the other way round; from the last chapter, we should know that this is a logical necessity as well:

$$\sim(x) \sim Fx \supset (Ez)Fz$$

"If it is not that case that everyone is not stupid, then there is someone who is stupid" obviously is a logical necessity.

$$\mathbf{F} \quad \sim(x) \sim Fx \supset (Ez)Fz$$

The material implication goes down first:

$$\mathbf{F} \quad \sim(x) \sim Fx \supset (Ez)Fz \ \checkmark$$
$$\mathbf{T} \quad \sim(x) \sim Fx$$
$$\mathbf{F} \quad (Ez)Fz$$

Now the only truth function outside the quantifiers:

$$\mathbf{F} \quad \sim(x) \sim Fx \supset (Ez)Fz \ \checkmark$$
$$\mathbf{T} \quad \sim(x) \sim Fx \ \checkmark$$
$$\mathbf{F} \quad (Ez)Fz$$
$$\mathbf{F} \quad (x) \sim Fx$$

The trick with doing logic like this is to think like a machine. Follow all the rules mechanically and you will not need to think; that is part of the point of logic.[3] The next thing a machine would do is bring down the false universal quantifier as that has a restriction on it:

$$\mathbf{F} \quad \sim(x) \sim Fx \supset (Ez)Fz \ \checkmark$$
$$\mathbf{T} \quad \sim(x) \sim Fx \ \checkmark$$
$$\mathbf{F} \quad (Ez)Fz$$
$$\mathbf{F} \quad (x) \sim Fx \ \checkmark$$
$$\mathbf{F} \quad \sim Fa$$

There has just appeared a truth function that is not bounded by a quantifier; we deal with itstraight away:

$$\mathbf{F} \quad \sim(x) \sim Fx \supset (Ez)Fz \ \checkmark$$
$$\mathbf{T} \quad \sim(x) \sim Fx \ \checkmark$$
$$\mathbf{F} \quad (Ez)Fz$$
$$\mathbf{F} \quad (x) \sim Fx \ \checkmark$$
$$\mathbf{F} \quad \sim Fa \checkmark$$
$$\mathbf{T} \quad Fa$$

There is only one line that has not been ticked and there is no restriction what letter we use when we bring it down. Whenever that happens, you should begin

---

[3]All the thinking has gone into the formulation and formalisation, the deduction being mechanised.

by bringing down a letter you have used already.

$$\begin{array}{ll}
\mathbf{F} & \sim(x) \sim Fx \supset (Ez)Fz \ \checkmark \\
\mathbf{T} & \sim(x) \sim Fx \ \checkmark \\
\mathbf{F} & (Ez)Fz \ \checkmark \\
\mathbf{F} & (x) \sim Fx \ \checkmark \\
\mathbf{F} & \sim Fa\checkmark \\
\mathbf{T} & Fa \\
\mathbf{F} & Fa
\end{array}$$

The sentence is a logical necessity, which is no surprise.

We have not yet seen a tableau that branches. A branching tableau in predicate logic is exactly the same as one for propositional logic except with the extra rules.

$$(y)(Fy \supset Gy) \supset \sim(Ex)(Fx \cdot \sim Gx)$$

From the last chapter you should recognize $(x)(Fx \supset Gx)$ as the **A** form sentence of a syllogism, it means every F is a G. So the above sentence means that every F is a G there is no F which is not G. Is this a logical necessity? First we assume it is false:

$$\mathbf{F} \quad (y)(Fy \supset Gy) \supset \sim(Ex)(Fx \cdot \sim Gx)$$

The next few steps are easy, the material implication (the main connective) goes first:

$$\begin{array}{ll}
\mathbf{F} & (y)(Fy \supset Gy) \supset \sim(Ex)(Fx \cdot \sim Gx) \ \checkmark \\
\mathbf{T} & (y)(Fy \supset Gy) \\
\mathbf{F} & \sim(Ex)(Fx \cdot \sim Gx)
\end{array}$$

Now we deal with all the truth functions:

$$\begin{array}{ll}
\mathbf{F} & (y)(Fy \supset Gy) \supset \sim(Ex)(Fx \cdot \sim Gx) \ \checkmark \\
\mathbf{T} & (y)(Fy \supset Gy) \\
\mathbf{F} & \sim(Ex)(Fx \cdot \sim Gx) \ \checkmark \\
\mathbf{T} & (Ex)(Fx \cdot \sim Gx)
\end{array}$$

Next we bring down the quantifiers with restrictions on them. There is only one: a true existential quantifier.

$$\begin{array}{ll}
\mathbf{F} & (y)(Fy \supset Gy) \supset \sim(Ex)(Fx \cdot \sim Gx) \ \checkmark \\
\mathbf{T} & (y)(Fy \supset Gy) \\
\mathbf{F} & \sim(Ex)(Fx \cdot \sim Gx) \ \checkmark \\
\mathbf{T} & (Ex)(Fx \cdot \sim Gx) \ \checkmark \\
\mathbf{T} & Fa \cdot \sim Ga)
\end{array}$$

Now the truth functions. The only truth function on an un-ticked line that is outside all the quantifiers on that line is a conjunction, it comes straight down:

$$
\begin{array}{ll}
\mathbf{F} & (y)(Fy \supset Gy) \supset \sim(Ex)(Fx \cdot \sim Gx) \ \checkmark \\
\mathbf{T} & (y)(Fy \supset Gy) \\
\mathbf{F} & \sim(Ex)(Fx \cdot \sim Gx) \ \checkmark \\
\mathbf{T} & (Ex)(Fx \cdot \sim Gx) \ \checkmark \\
\mathbf{T} & Fa \cdot \sim Ga \checkmark \\
\mathbf{T} & Fa \\
\mathbf{T} & \sim Ga
\end{array}
$$

There are still truth functions to deal with:

$$
\begin{array}{ll}
\mathbf{F} & (y)(Fy \supset Gy) \supset \sim(Ex)(Fx \cdot \sim Gx) \ \checkmark \\
\mathbf{T} & (y)(Fy \supset Gy) \\
\mathbf{F} & \sim(Ex)(Fx \cdot \sim Gx) \ \checkmark \\
\mathbf{T} & (Ex)(Fx \cdot \sim Gx) \ \checkmark \\
\mathbf{T} & Fa \cdot \sim Ga \checkmark \\
\mathbf{T} & Fa \\
\mathbf{T} & \sim Ga \ \checkmark \\
\mathbf{F} & Ga
\end{array}
$$

Now the last unticked line:

$$
\begin{array}{ll}
\mathbf{F} & (y)(Fy \supset Gy) \supset \sim(Ex)(Fx \cdot \sim Gx) \ \checkmark \\
\mathbf{T} & (y)(Fy \supset Gy) \ \checkmark \\
\mathbf{F} & \sim(Ex)(Fx \cdot \sim Gx) \ \checkmark \\
\mathbf{T} & (Ex)(Fx \cdot \sim Gx) \ \checkmark \\
\mathbf{T} & Fa \cdot \sim Ga \checkmark \\
\mathbf{T} & Fa \\
\mathbf{T} & \sim Ga \ \checkmark \\
\mathbf{F} & Ga \\
\mathbf{T} & Fa \supset Ga
\end{array}
$$

The only unticked line is a true material implication, this will branch:

$$
\begin{array}{ll}
\mathbf{F} & (y)(Fy \supset Gy) \supset \sim(Ex)(Fx \cdot \sim Gx) \ \checkmark \\
\mathbf{T} & (y)(Fy \supset Gy) \ \checkmark \\
\mathbf{F} & \sim(Ex)(Fx \cdot \sim Gx) \ \checkmark \\
\mathbf{T} & (Ex)(Fx \cdot \sim Gx) \ \checkmark \\
\mathbf{T} & Fa \cdot \sim Ga \checkmark \\
\mathbf{T} & Fa \\
\mathbf{T} & \sim Ga \ \checkmark \\
\mathbf{F} & Ga \\
\mathbf{T} & Fa \supset Ga \ \checkmark
\end{array}
$$

$$
\begin{array}{ccc}
& \diagup \quad \diagdown & \\
\mathbf{F} \ \ Fa & & \mathbf{T} \ \ Ga \\
\times & & \times
\end{array}
$$

The sentence is a logical necessity, it should be clear what is contradicting with what. Here is the same sentence with the material implication the other way round.[4]

$$\textbf{F} \quad \sim(Ex)(Fx \cdot \sim Gx) \supset (y)(Fy \supset Gy)$$

$\textbf{F} \quad \sim(Ex)(Fx \cdot \sim Gx) \supset (y)(Fy \supset Gy) \checkmark$
$\textbf{T} \quad \sim(Ex)(Fx \cdot \sim Gx)$
$\textbf{F} \quad (y)(Fy \supset Gy)$

$\textbf{F} \quad \sim(Ex)(Fx \cdot \sim Gx) \supset (y)(Fy \supset Gy) \checkmark$
$\textbf{T} \quad \sim(Ex)(Fx \cdot \sim Gx) \checkmark$
$\textbf{F} \quad (y)(Fy \supset Gy)$
$\textbf{F} \quad (Ex)(Fx \cdot \sim Gx)$

The quantifier to bring down first is the one with the restriction on it, the false universal quantifier:

$\textbf{F} \quad \sim(Ex)(Fx \cdot \sim Gx) \supset (y)(Fy \supset Gy) \checkmark$
$\textbf{T} \quad \sim(Ex)(Fx \cdot \sim Gx) \checkmark$
$\textbf{F} \quad (y)(Fy \supset Gy) \checkmark$
$\textbf{F} \quad (Ex)(Fx \cdot \sim Gx)$
$\textbf{F} \quad Fa \supset Ga$

Now the truth function we have freed from the clutches of the universal quantifier should be dealt with before we do the other quantifier.

$\textbf{F} \quad \sim(Ex)(Fx \cdot \sim Gx) \supset (y)(Fy \supset Gy) \checkmark$
$\textbf{T} \quad \sim(Ex)(Fx \cdot \sim Gx) \checkmark$
$\textbf{F} \quad (y)(Fy \supset Gy) \checkmark$
$\textbf{F} \quad (Ex)(Fx \cdot \sim Gx)$
$\textbf{F} \quad Fa \supset Ga \checkmark$
$\textbf{T} \quad Fa$
$\textbf{F} \quad Ga$

Now it is the turn of the other quantifier, because it is the only remaining unticked line. As it is a false existential quantifier there is no restriction on what letter you use. It really is a good idea to choose a letter you have used already:

---

[4]If the sentence had been like this:

$$(y)(Fy \supset Gy) \equiv \sim(Ex)(Fx \cdot \sim Gx)$$

then in order to prove it is a logical necessity, you would rewrite it as two sentences, one with a material implication instead of the material equivalence and the other with the material implication reversed. If both the sentences are valid then the entire sentence (with the material equivalence) is valid. See also the method of Section 11.3.

$$\begin{array}{ll} \text{F} & \sim(Ex)(Fx \cdot \sim Gx) \supset (y)(Fy \supset Gy) \ \checkmark \\ \text{T} & \sim(Ex)(Fx \cdot \sim Gx) \ \checkmark \\ \text{F} & (y)(Fy \supset Gy) \ \checkmark \\ \text{F} & (Ex)(Fx \cdot \sim Gx) \ \checkmark \\ \text{F} & Fa \supset Ga \ \checkmark \\ \text{T} & Fa \\ \text{F} & Ga \\ \text{F} & Fa \cdot \sim Ga \end{array}$$

The only remaining line branches, since it is a false conjunction:

$$\begin{array}{ll} \text{F} & \sim(Ex)(Fx \cdot \sim Gx) \supset (y)(Fy \supset Gy) \ \checkmark \\ \text{T} & \sim(Ex)(Fx \cdot \sim Gx) \ \checkmark \\ \text{F} & (y)(Fy \supset Gy) \ \checkmark \\ \text{F} & (Ex)(Fx \cdot \sim Gx) \ \checkmark \\ \text{F} & Fa \supset Ga \ \checkmark \\ \text{T} & Fa \\ \text{F} & Ga \\ \text{F} & Fa \cdot \sim Ga \ \checkmark \end{array}$$

$$\begin{array}{ccc} & \diagup & \diagdown \\ \text{F} \quad Fa & & \text{F} \quad \sim Ga \\ \times & & \end{array}$$

Now the very last step:

$$\begin{array}{ll} \text{F} & \sim(Ex)(Fx \cdot \sim Gx) \supset (y)(Fy \supset Gy) \ \checkmark \\ \text{T} & \sim(Ex)(Fx \cdot \sim Gx) \ \checkmark \\ \text{F} & (y)(Fy \supset Gy) \ \checkmark \\ \text{F} & (Ex)(Fx \cdot \sim Gx) \ \checkmark \\ \text{F} & Fa \supset Ga \ \checkmark \\ \text{T} & Fa \\ \text{F} & Ga \\ \text{F} & Fa \cdot \sim Ga \ \checkmark \end{array}$$

$$\begin{array}{ccc} & \diagup & \diagdown \\ \text{F} \quad Fa & & \text{F} \quad \sim Ga \ \checkmark \\ \times & & \text{T} \quad Ga \\ & & \times \end{array}$$

11.3   Choice of variables

It does not matter what variables you have in your sentence. When the quantifiers are separated, you can use whatever letters you like for the variables, even the same ones:

$$(x)Fx \equiv (y)Fy$$

Here is a nice quick way of dealing with a material equivalence in a tableau:

$$\textbf{F} \quad (x)Fx \equiv (y)Fy$$

When a material equivalence is false it means that one of the sentences is true and the other is false. We can write that like this:

$$\textbf{F} \quad (x)Fx \equiv (y)Fy \ \checkmark$$

T	$(x)Fx$	**F**	$(x)Fx$
F	$(y)Fy$	**T**	$(y)Fy$

In each line we should bring down the false universal first as there is a restriction on it:

$$\textbf{F} \quad (x)Fx \equiv (y)Fy \ \checkmark$$

T	$(x)Fx$	**F**	$(x)Fx \ \checkmark$
F	$(y)Fy \ \checkmark$	**T**	$(y)Fy$
F	Fa	**F**	Fa

Now the last lines to hit a contradiction in both branches:

$$\textbf{F} \quad (x)Fx \equiv (y)Fy \ \checkmark$$

T	$(x)Fx \ \checkmark$	**F**	$(x)Fx \ \checkmark$
F	$(y)Fy \ \checkmark$	**T**	$(y)Fy \ \checkmark$
F	Fa	**F**	Fa
T	Fa	**T**	Fa
	✕		✕

Exactly the same sort of setup happens for the same sentence with existential quantifiers:

$$(Ex)Fx \equiv (Ey)Fy$$

Here is the completed tableau:

$$\textbf{F} \quad (Ex)Fx \equiv (Ey)Fy \ \checkmark$$

T	$(Ex)Fx \ \checkmark$	**F**	$(Ex)Fx \ \checkmark$
F	$(Ey)Fy \ \checkmark$	**T**	$(Ey)Fy \ \checkmark$
T	Fa	**T**	Fa
F	Fa	**F**	Fa
	✕		✕

The only time you must keep your quantifier variables different (i.e. must adhere to the variable convention) is when one quantifier is in the scope of the other. For example:

$$(x)(Ey)Lxy$$

Here, the variables must be different.

$$(x)(Fx \supset (Ey)(Gy \cdot Lxy))$$

If this sentence is to mean, say, every man loves a woman[5] then the variable letters must be kept different.

Here is a sentence that breaches the variable convention, notice that no harm is done. Although the two quantifiers use the same letter, the tableau runs as it would if they used different letters.

$$(x)(Fx \supset Gx) \equiv (x)(\sim Gx \supset \sim Fx)$$

It should be clear that this sentence is a logical necessity. The left reads "All Fs are G," the right reads "All non-Gs are not Fs." The two sentences are logically equivalent. The main connective is a material equivalence ($\equiv$) so to prove it is a logical necessity we will split it into two sentences and deal with each one separately:

1. $(x)(Fx \supset Gx) \supset (x)(\sim Gx \supset \sim Fx)$

2. $(x)(\sim Gx \supset \sim Fx) \supset (x)(Fx \supset Gx)$

Here is a tableau for the first:

$$\mathbf{F} \quad (x)(Fx \supset Gx) \supset (x)(\sim Gx \supset \sim Fx)$$

$\mathbf{F} \quad (x)(Fx \supset Gx) \supset (x)(\sim Gx \supset \sim Fx) \; \surd$
$\mathbf{T} \quad (x)(Fx \supset Gx)$
$\mathbf{F} \quad (x)(\sim Gx \supset \sim Fx)$

The first one to bring down is the false universal quantifier as that has a restriction on what letter you can bring down:

$\mathbf{F} \quad (x)(Fx \supset Gx) \supset (x)(\sim Gx \supset \sim Fx) \; \surd$
$\mathbf{T} \quad (x)(Fx \supset Gx)$
$\mathbf{F} \quad (x)(\sim Gx \supset \sim Fx) \; \surd$
$\mathbf{F} \quad \sim Ga \supset \sim Fa$

$\mathbf{F} \quad (x)(Fx \supset Gx) \supset (x)(\sim Gx \supset \sim Fx) \; \surd$
$\mathbf{T} \quad (x)(Fx \supset Gx)$
$\mathbf{F} \quad (x)(\sim Gx \supset \sim Fx) \; \surd$
$\mathbf{F} \quad \sim Ga \supset \sim Fa \; \surd$
$\mathbf{T} \quad \sim Ga$
$\mathbf{F} \quad \sim Fa$

[5] For every x, if x is a man then there is a y that is a woman and x loves y.

I will do the next two steps (eliminating the two negations on the bottom two rows) in one go. Technically, there is no rule allowing the bringing down of two lines at the same time, so in general it should not be done.

$$
\begin{array}{ll}
\textbf{F} & (x)(Fx \supset Gx) \supset (x)(\sim Gx \supset \sim Fx) \ \checkmark \\
\textbf{T} & (x)(Fx \supset Gx) \\
\textbf{F} & (x)(\sim Gx \supset \sim Fx) \ \checkmark \\
\textbf{F} & \sim Ga \supset \sim Fa \ \checkmark \\
\textbf{T} & \sim Ga \ \checkmark \\
\textbf{F} & \sim Fa \ \checkmark \\
\textbf{F} & Ga \\
\textbf{T} & Fa
\end{array}
$$

Now to bring down the true universal quantifier (the only line un-ticked that can be brought down):

$$
\begin{array}{ll}
\textbf{F} & (x)(Fx \supset Gx) \supset (x)(\sim Gx \supset \sim Fx) \ \checkmark \\
\textbf{T} & (x)(Fx \supset Gx) \ \checkmark \\
\textbf{F} & (x)(\sim Gx \supset \sim Fx) \ \checkmark \\
\textbf{F} & \sim Ga \supset \sim Fa \ \checkmark \\
\textbf{T} & \sim Ga \ \checkmark \\
\textbf{F} & \sim Fa \ \checkmark \\
\textbf{F} & Ga \\
\textbf{T} & Fa \\
\textbf{T} & Fa \supset Ga
\end{array}
$$

The last step will involve branching, since the truth function is a material implication, and it is true:

$$
\begin{array}{ll}
\textbf{F} & (x)(Fx \supset Gx) \supset (x)(\sim Gx \supset \sim Fx) \ \checkmark \\
\textbf{T} & (x)(Fx \supset Gx) \ \checkmark \\
\textbf{F} & (x)(\sim Gx \supset \sim Fx) \ \checkmark \\
\textbf{F} & \sim Ga \supset \sim Fa \ \checkmark \\
\textbf{T} & \sim Ga \ \checkmark \\
\textbf{F} & \sim Fa \ \checkmark \\
\textbf{F} & Ga \\
\textbf{T} & Fa \\
\textbf{T} & Fa \supset Ga \ \checkmark
\end{array}
$$

$$
\begin{array}{cc}
\textbf{F} \ \ Fa & \textbf{T} \ \ Ga \\
\times & \times
\end{array}
$$

Here is a completed tableau for the material implication going the other way:

$$
\begin{array}{ll}
\text{F} & (x)(\sim\!Gx \supset \sim\!Fx) \supset (x)(Fx \supset Gx) \ \checkmark \\
\text{T} & (x)(\sim\!Gx \supset \sim\!Fx) \ \checkmark \\
\text{F} & (x)(Fx \supset Gx) \ \checkmark \\
\text{F} & \sim\!Fa \supset Ga \ \checkmark \\
\text{T} & Fa \\
\text{F} & Ga \\
\text{T} & \sim\!Ga \supset \sim\!Fa \ \checkmark
\end{array}
$$

$$
\begin{array}{cc}
\text{F} \quad \sim\!Ga \ \checkmark & \text{T} \quad \sim\!Fa \ \checkmark \\
\text{T} \quad Ga & \text{F} \quad Fa \\
\times & \times
\end{array}
$$

11.4   Exercises

Use the tableau method to verify that the following are logically necessary. You may need to bring down some lines more than once.[6]

1. $(x)(Fx \supset Gx) \supset (y) \sim (Fy \cdot \sim\!Gy)$

2. $(Ex)(Fx \cdot \sim\!Gx) \supset \sim(y) \sim (Fy \supset Gy)$

3. $(x)(y)Fxy \supset (y)(x)Fxy$

4. $[(x)Fx \cdot (Ey)Gy] \supset (Ez)(Fz \cdot Gz)$

5. $(y)(Fy \vee Gy) \supset [(Ex) \sim Fx \supset (Ez)Gz]$

6. $(x)(Fx) \supset (Fa \cdot Fb)$

7. $(y)(Fy \supset Gy) \supset [(Ex)Fx \supset (Ez)Gz]$

8. $(x)(Fx \supset Ga) \supset [(Ex)Fx \supset Ga]$

9. $(z) \sim Hza \supset (Haa \supset Gb)$

10. $(Ex)(y)(Fx \cdot \sim\!Fy) \supset (z)(Gz)$

11. $(Ex)(Fx \supset (y)Fy)$

12. $(Ex)((Ey)Fy \supset Fx)$

13. $(\sim\!Fa \supset Fb) \supset (Ex)Fx$

---

[6]Thanks to P. Alexander for his data retrieval and delivery skills.

11.5   Arguments in predicate logic

11.5.1   The standard arguments

Arguments in predicate logic, surprisingly enough, are treated in exactly the same way as an argument in propositional logic.

Here is a famous argument:

> All men are mortal
> <u>Socrates is a man</u>
> Socrates is mortal

The first thing to do is translate the argument into predicate logic. This should be very easy (we did an argument similar to this at the end of the last chapter).

$(x)(Hx \supset Mx)$ <u>Key</u>
$\underline{Ha}$ $\overline{H} = \ldots$ is a man
Ma $M = \ldots$ is mortal
                               $a = $ Socrates

To prove it, we assume the premises are true and the conclusion is false and derive a contradiction:

$$\begin{array}{ll} \mathbf{T} & (x)(Hx \supset Mx) \\ \mathbf{T} & \underline{Ha} \\ \mathbf{F} & Ma \end{array}$$

There is only one line we can bring down. There is no restriction on what letter we use:

$$\begin{array}{ll} \mathbf{T} & (x)(Hx \supset Mx) \;\checkmark \\ \mathbf{T} & \underline{Ha} \\ \mathbf{F} & Ma \\ \mathbf{T} & Ha \supset Ma \end{array}$$

There is only one line and that branches:

$$\begin{array}{ll} \mathbf{T} & (x)(Hx \supset Mx) \;\checkmark \\ \mathbf{T} & \underline{Ha} \\ \mathbf{F} & Ma \\ \mathbf{T} & Ha \supset Ma \;\checkmark \end{array}$$

$$\begin{array}{ccc} \mathbf{F}\;\; Ha & & \mathbf{T}\;\; Ma \\ \times & & \times \end{array}$$

Every branch has hit a contradiction the argument is valid.

Here is another argument that is just as famous:

$$(x)(Cx \supset Mx)$$
$$(x)(Mx \supset Vx)$$
$$\overline{(x)(Cx \supset Vx)}$$

Key
$C = \ldots$ is a cat
$M = \ldots$ is mammal
$V = \ldots$ is a vertebrate

The first step is familiar:

T $(x)(Cx \supset Mx)$
T $(x)(Mx \supset Vx)$
F $(x)(Cx \supset Vx)$

The first line to bring down is the false universal quantifier as that has a restriction on what letters you can pick when bringing it down (the restriction is not to choose any letters that have appeared before).

T $(x)(Cx \supset Mx)$
T $(x)(Mx \supset Vx)$
F $(x)(Cx \supset Vx)$ $\checkmark$
F $Ca \supset Va$

Next the unbound truth function:

T $(x)(Cx \supset Mx)$
T $(x)(Mx \supset Vx)$
F $(x)(Cx \supset Vx)$ $\checkmark$
F $Ca \supset Va$
T Ca
F Va

Next, one of the premises should come down. Both are true universal quantifiers (no restriction), so it makes no difference which comes down first:

T $(x)(Cx \supset Mx)$ $\checkmark$
T $(x)(Mx \supset Vx)$
F $(x)(Cx \supset Vx)$ $\checkmark$
F $Ca \supset Va$
T Ca
F Va
T $Ca \supset Ma$

Now the truth function:

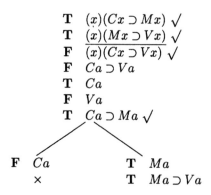

We bring down the next premise, on which there is no restriction (as the main connective is a true universal qantifier).

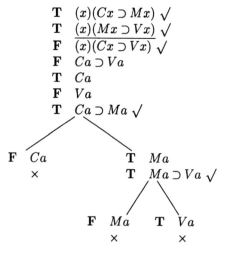

Now the last unticked line:

Once you have got the hang of all the rules this really is quite easy.

11.5.2 Arguments with multiple quantifiers

Here is a slightly more complicated argument:

All the world loves a lover
<u>Romeo loves Juliet</u>
Iago loves Desdemona

Taken in a very literal way (which is the only way our logic is going to do it), the argument is in fact valid.

- Romeo loves Juliet.

- Therefore Romeo is a lover.

- All the world loves a lover, but Romeo is a lover.

- So all the world loves Romeo.

- Thus everyone in the world is a lover (as they all love Romeo).

- But everyone in the world loves a lover and everyone in the world is a lover.

- Everyone in the world loves everyone else.

- So Iago loves Desdemona.

The argument is valid, here is how it formalizes:

$(x)(\ (Ey)Lxy \supset (z)(Lzx)\ )^7$ Key
<u>Lab</u> $\overline{L = \ldots \text{loves} \ldots}$
Lcd $a = \text{Romeo}$
                       $b = \text{Juliet}$
                       $c = \text{Iago}$
                       $d = \text{Desdemona}$

Here is how to validate this argument in Predicate Logic:

T $(x)(\ (Ey)Lxy \supset (z)(Lzx)\ )$
T   <u>Lab</u>
F Lcd

There is only one line that it is possible to bring down. What is different here is that we are spoilt for choice as to which name to use. I will use the a:

T $(x)(\ (Ey)Lxy \supset (z)(Lzx)\ )$ $\checkmark$
T   <u>Lab</u>
F Lcd
T $(Ey)Lay \supset (z)(Lza)$

---

[7]$(x)(\ (Ey)Lxy \supset (z)(Lzx)\ )$ means that for any person, if there is a person that they love then everyone loves them.

Now we deal with the material implication (it is not held inside the brackets of any quantifier):

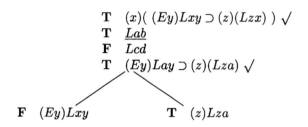

On none of the branches are we restricted as to which name to use. On the left branch, we can get a contradiction instantly if we use a b:

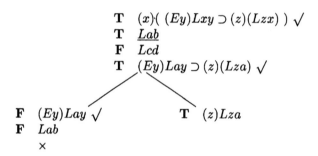

We cannot produce a contradiction immediately on the right hand branch, so we will have to use a line more than once. The quickest way to hit a contradiction is to choose a d for the right column:

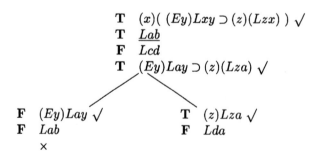

There is only one line worth bringing down again, the line just before the branch. Note that we cannot use the line **F** $(Ey)Lay$ because it is on another branch. The only lines that are accessible for re-use are the ones above in the same branch (going all the way up to the top of the tableau).

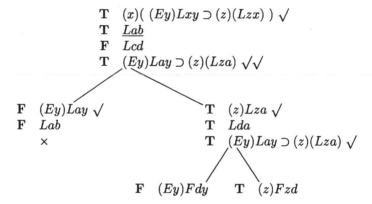

We split up the truth function.[8]

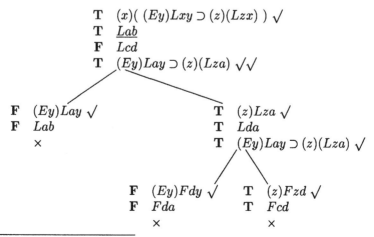

Now it it is possible to generate contradictions on the remaining two branches. We use an a for the left and a c for the right, we can close the tableau.

T $(x)(\ (Ey)Lxy \supset (z)(Lzx)\ )$ ✓
T   <u>Lab</u>
F Lcd
T $(Ey)Lay \supset (z)(Lza)$ ✓✓

F $(Ey)Lay$ ✓   T $(z)Lza$ ✓
F Lab T Lda
×   T $(Ey)Lay \supset (z)(Lza)$ ✓

                    F $(Ey)Fdy$ ✓   T $(z)Fzd$ ✓
                    F Fda T Fcd
                    ×   ×

---

[8]Note that when we use a line again we do not have to rewrite it, we may just bring it down the branch a second time. In this example I rewrite the sentence for a little clarity.

You would be unlucky to have to produce a tableau as complicated as this, unless you get seriously interested in logic. Even then, nowadays a computer would do it for you.

Here is another argument which will use lots of quantifiers:

> Someone hates everyone
> Anyone who is hated is unhappy
> ―――――――――――――――――
> Everyone is unhappy

Thinking about it, this argument is valid: everybody is hated, so everyone is unhappy. Here is the formalisation:

$(Ex)(y)Hxy$ Key

$(x)(\ (Ey)Hyx \supset Ux\ )$ $H = \ldots$ hates $\ldots$

――――――――――――――

$(x)Ux$ $U = \ldots$ is unhappy

The first step is to assume that the premises are true and the conlusion is false:

$$\begin{array}{ll} \mathbf{T} & (Ex)(y)Hxy \\ \mathbf{T} & (x)(\ (Ey)Hyx \supset Ux\ ) \\ \mathbf{F} & (x)Ux \end{array}$$

First of all, we deal with the two lines that have restrictions on them. I will do the one with the fewest quantifiers around it (the simplest one):

$$\begin{array}{ll} \mathbf{T} & (Ex)(y)Hxy \\ \mathbf{T} & (x)(\ (Ey)Hyx \supset Ux\ ) \\ \mathbf{F} & (x)Ux \ \sqrt{} \\ \mathbf{F} & Ua \end{array}$$

Now for the next one (the top row). When dealing with sentences involving multiple quantifiers like that, you MUST always do the leftmost ones first. This is a law of the tableau system.[9] We have already used the letter a as a name so we cannot use it when bring down this true existential quantifier:

$$\begin{array}{ll} \mathbf{T} & (Ex)(y)Hxy \ \sqrt{} \\ \mathbf{T} & (x)(\ (Ey)Hyx \supset Ux\ ) \\ \mathbf{F} & (x)Ux \ \sqrt{} \\ \mathbf{F} & Ua \\ \mathbf{T} & (y)Hby \end{array}$$

There is no restriction on any of the remaining quantifiers, I shall bring down the simplest first. Once again it is a good idea to use names we have already used, I will use an a.

―――――――――――――――

[9]Remember that a quantifier should be brought down only when it has become the *main connective*; when it is not in the scope of any truth functions or other quantifiers.

$$\begin{array}{ll} \mathbf{T} & (Ex)(y)Hxy \ \checkmark \\ \mathbf{T} & (x)(\ (Ey)Hyx \supset Ux\ ) \\ \mathbf{F} & \underline{(x)Ux\ \checkmark} \\ \mathbf{F} & Ua \\ \mathbf{T} & (y)Hby\ \checkmark \\ \mathbf{T} & Hba \end{array}$$

There is only one line left to bring down. If you look at it, you will see a Ux on the far right. Since we alredy have Ua it would be a good idea to bring the x down as an a:

$$\begin{array}{ll} \mathbf{T} & (Ex)(y)Hxy \ \checkmark \\ \mathbf{T} & (x)(\ (Ey)Hyx \supset Ux\ )\ \checkmark \\ \mathbf{F} & \underline{(x)Ux\ \checkmark} \\ \mathbf{F} & Ua \\ \mathbf{T} & (y)Hby\ \checkmark \\ \mathbf{T} & Hba \\ \mathbf{T} & (Ey)Hya \supset Ua \end{array}$$

Now we have to get rid of the material implication, in doing so we hit a contradiction on one of the branches.

$$\begin{array}{ll} \mathbf{T} & (Ex)(y)Hxy \ \checkmark \\ \mathbf{T} & (x)(\ (Ey)Hyx \supset Ux\ )\ \checkmark \\ \mathbf{F} & \underline{(x)Ux\ \checkmark} \\ \mathbf{F} & Ua \\ \mathbf{T} & (y)Hby\ \checkmark \\ \mathbf{T} & Hba \\ \mathbf{T} & (Ey)Hya \supset Ua\ \checkmark \end{array}$$

$$\begin{array}{ccc} \mathbf{F}\ (Ey)Hya & & \mathbf{T}\ Ua \\ & & \times \end{array}$$

It should be clear what to do for the last step.

$$\begin{array}{ll} \mathbf{T} & (Ex)(y)Hxy \ \checkmark \\ \mathbf{T} & (x)(\ (Ey)Hyx \supset Ux\ )\ \checkmark \\ \mathbf{F} & \underline{(x)Ux\ \checkmark} \\ \mathbf{F} & Ua \\ \mathbf{T} & (y)Hby\ \checkmark \\ \mathbf{T} & Hba \\ \mathbf{T} & (Ey)Hya \supset Ua\ \checkmark \end{array}$$

$$\begin{array}{ccc} \mathbf{F}\ (Ey)Hya\ \checkmark & & \mathbf{T}\ Ua \\ \mathbf{F}\ Hba & & \times \\ \times & & \end{array}$$

Here is one final argument for which I will write the formalisation:

$$(x)(Ey)(z)(Hxyz \lor [(Ev)(Gvz \cdot Gvy)]) \supset (x) \sim (y)(Hxxy \lor Hyyx)$$
$$(x)(Ey)(z)(Hxyz \lor [(Ev)(Gvz \cdot Gvy)])$$
$$\overline{(x) \sim (y)(Hxxy \lor Hyyx)}$$

The way to deal with this argument is very simple. Keeping in mind that a sentence written in formal logic is still a sentence, we do this:

$A \supset B$ Key

$\underline{A}$ $A = (x)(Ey)(z)(Hxyz \lor [(Ev)(Gvz \cdot Gvy)])$

B $B = (x) \sim (y)(Hxxy \lor Hyyx)$

Now we have Modus Ponens in propositional logic.

11.6   Exercises

By the tableau method, show that the following are valid arguments.

1. $(x)(Fx \supset Gx)$
$\underline{(Ex)(Fx \cdot Hx)}$
$(Ex)(Gx \cdot Hx)$

2. $(x)(Fx \supset \sim Gx)$
$\underline{(x)(Hx \supset Gx)}$
$(x)(Hx \supset \sim Fx)$

3. $(x)(Fx \supset \sim Gx)$
$\underline{(Ex)(Hx \cdot Fx)}$
$(Ex)(Hx \cdot \sim Gx)$

4. $\dfrac{(x)(Fx \supset Hx)}{(x)[\,(Ey)(Gy \cdot Kxy) \supset (Ez)(Hz \cdot Kxz)\,]}$

5. $(x)[(Fx \lor Gx) \supset Hx]$
$\underline{(Ex)(Fx \cdot Jx)}$
$(Ex)Hx$

6. $(x)(Fx \supset Gx)$
$(x)(Hx \supset Jx)$
$\underline{(Ex)(Fx \lor Hx)}$
$(Ex)(Gx \lor Jx)$

7. $(x)[Fx \equiv (Ey)(Gy \cdot Kxy)]$
$\underline{(x)(Hx \supset Gx)}$
$(Ex)(Ey)(Hy \cdot Kxy) \supset (Ex)(Fx)$

8. $(x)(y)[(Fx \cdot Gy) \supset Kxy]$
$\underline{(x)(Ey)(Lxy \supset Fx)}$
$(x)(Ey)[(Lxy \cdot Gy) \supset Kxy]$

9. Suppose that F represents the predicate "...is an athlete," G represents the predicate "...is a foot," H represents the predicate "...is unwashed" and K represents the predicate "...has ...." Express in English the arguments 1–6 represent.

11.7 Identity

11.7.1 Identity and more new rules

An extremely useful extension of Predicate Logic is Predicate iogic with identity, which is able to express identities between objects. The difference between this predicate and all other predicates is that special rules for identity are added to the logic.

We would like to make an inference like this:

$$a = b$$
$$\underline{b = c}$$
$$a = c$$

In normal predicate logic if we treat the $=$ just like any other predicate, the argument will come out as invalid. However we know that if a is the same as b and b is the same as c then a is the same as c. In order to make deductions about identity work properly we add some extra rules to the deduction system. Here are the extra deduction rules for the tableau system:

Definition 11.7.1

1. *At any point in the tableau we can write down (from nowhere) the line* **T** $a = a$ *or* **T** $b = b$ *or* **T** $c = c$.... *In other words, at any point in the tableau we can say that an object is equal to itself.*[10]

2. *If a line like* **T** $a = b$ *turns up in the tableau then at any point in the tableau after that line, a and the b are interchangeable.*

Here are the two rules in action:
The very simple sentence $a = a$ is a logical necessity. Here is the tableau:

$$\mathbf{F} \quad a = a$$

We can use the first rule and put as the next line the sentence "**T** $a = a$" thus generating a contradiction.

$$\mathbf{F} \quad a = a$$
$$\mathbf{T} \quad a = a$$
$$\times$$

---

[10]This is the tableau version of Leibniz' law: identical objects have the same predicates (are indistinguishable).

The above illustrates the *reflexivity of identity*. Here is another argument that uses rule two.

$$\begin{array}{ll}\mathbf{T} & a = b \\ \mathbf{T} & \underline{b = c} \\ \mathbf{F} & a = c\end{array}$$

Using the second rule we can interchange the b on the second line for an a, because on the first line there is a true $a = b$, thus closing the tableau.

$$\begin{array}{ll}\mathbf{T} & a = b \\ \mathbf{T} & \underline{b = c}\ \checkmark \\ \mathbf{F} & a = c \\ \mathbf{T} & a = c \\ & \times\end{array}$$

The above shows the *transitivity of identity*. Here is another argument that uses both the new rules:

$$\begin{array}{ll}\mathbf{T} & \underline{a = b} \\ \mathbf{F} & b = a\end{array}$$

From the first rule we can substitute the b in the second line for an a, since in the first line there is a line like this $\mathbf{T}\ a = b$:

$$\begin{array}{ll}\mathbf{T} & \underline{a = b} \\ \mathbf{F} & b = a\ \checkmark \\ \mathbf{F} & a = a\end{array}$$

Now we use the first rule to finish the tableau:

$$\begin{array}{ll}\mathbf{T} & \underline{a = b} \\ \mathbf{F} & b = a\ \checkmark \\ \mathbf{F} & a = a \\ \mathbf{T} & a = a \\ & \times\end{array}$$

The tableau shows the *symmetry of identity*.

Identity is a very important and not at all trivial relation; it adds much power to our logic.

11.7.2   Identity for sentences of quantity

Sentences like this can be expressed in predicate logic with identity[11] which could not be expressed without identity:

1. There exists at least one idiot.

---

[11] Also known as CQC= meaning classical quantifier calculus with identity.

2. There are at least n good songs by dIRE sTRAITS (where n is any finite number).

3. There is at most one seriously groovy logic book.

4. There are at most two cops in Miami.

5. There are exactly two professionals.

Writing these in predicate logic is quite easy (but a little tedious). Here are some examples:

11.7.3 There is at least...

There is at least one idiot

Key
$I = \ldots$ is an idiot

$$(Ex)Ix$$

There are at least two idiots

Key
$I = \ldots$ is an idiot

$$(Ex)(Ey)(Ix \cdot Iy \cdot x \neq y)^{12}$$

The above formalisation reads as simply: there is an x and there is a y both of whom are idiots and x is non equal to y (or x is not the same as y).

There are at least three idiots

Key

$$(Ex)(Ey)(Ez)(Ix \cdot Iy \cdot Iz \cdot x \neq y \cdot x \neq z \cdot y \neq z)$$

$I = \ldots$ is an idiot

There are at least two stupid professors

Key
$S = \ldots$ is stupid
$I = \ldots$ is a professor

$$(Ex)(Ey)(Ix \cdot Iy \cdot Sx \cdot Sy \cdot x \neq y)$$

11.7.4 There are at most...

There exists at most one environmentalist

Key
$N = \ldots$ is an environmentalist

$$(x)(y)((Nx \cdot Ny) \supset x = y)$$

---

[12] $(x \neq y)$ is short for $\sim(x = y)$.

The above formalisation reads like this: for any two objects (for all x and for all y), if they are both environmentalists then they are really the same object."

There exists at most two environmentalists

Key

$$(x)(y)(z)((Nx \cdot Ny \cdot Nz) \supset (x = y \lor x = z \lor z = y))$$

$N = \ldots$ is an environmentalist

For any three objects, if they are all environmentalists, then two of them are the same (either the first is the same as the second, or the first is the same as the third, or the second is the same as the third).

There exists at most one clever environmentalist

Key

$$(x)(y)((Nx \cdot Ny \cdot Cx \cdot Cy) \supset x = y)^{13}$$

$N = \ldots$ is an environmentalist

$C = \ldots$ is clever

There are at most two balls

Key

$$(x)(y)(z)((Bx \cdot By \cdot Bz) \supset (x = y \lor x = z \lor y = z))$$

$B = \ldots$ is a ball

More literally: for any three objects, if they are all balls then at least two of them are the same (either the first really is the second, the first is the third or the second is the third).

11.7.5   There are exactly...

For a sentence like "there is exactly one blah" we take the conjunction of "there is at least one blah" and "there is at most one blah." Likewise, to say a statement like "there are exactly two blah" we make a conjunction of "there is at least two blah" and "there is at most two blah."

Exactly one student likes a (at least one) book

$$(Ex)(Sx \cdot (Ey)(By \cdot Lxy)) \cdot (x)(y)[(Sx \cdot (Ez)(Bz \cdot Lxz) \cdot Sy \cdot (Ev)(Bv \cdot Lxv)) \supset (x = y)]$$

Key

$S = \ldots$ a student

$B = \ldots$ is a book

$L = \ldots$ likes...

There is, however, is an easier way:

---

[13] It is a common mistake to do this:

There exists at most one clever environmentalist

Key

$$(x)(y)(((Nx \supset Cx) \cdot (Ny \supset Cy)) \supset x = y)$$

$N = \ldots$ is an environmentalist

$C = \ldots$ is clever

This means that there is at most one person who is a non-clever non-environmentalist.

There is exactly one elephant

Key $(Ex)(Hx \cdot (y)(Hy \supset y = x))$
$H = \ldots$ is an elephant

There is an elephant, and all elephants are it.

There are exactly two clever students

$$(Ex)(Ey)[(Sx \cdot Cx \cdot Sy \cdot Cy \cdot x \neq y) \cdot (z)((Sz \cdot Cz) \supset (z = x \vee z = y))]$$

Key
$S = \ldots$ a student
$C = \ldots$ is clever

There are two different clever students, and any [other] clever student is really one of them.

Here is a useful piece of information. Occasionally you will come across this quantifier: $(\exists!x)$. This is standard notation for "there exists exactly one. ..." Here is another way of formalising an "there is exactly one":

There is exactly one white elephant

Key $(Ey)(x)((Hx \cdot Wx) \equiv x = y)$
$H = \ldots$ is an elephant
$W = \ldots$ is white

Can you work this one out?

There are exactly two elephants

Key $(Ey)(Ez)[y \neq z \cdot (x)(Ux \equiv (x = y \vee x = z))]$
$H = \ldots$ is an elephant

Try to show by means of a large tableau that the following is a logical necessity:

$$(Ey)(x)(Hx \equiv x = y) \equiv (Ex)(Hx \cdot (y)(Hy \supset y = x))$$

11.8 Exercises

Express in predicate logic with identity the following. Verify, by means of a tableau, that 12 is a logical necessity.

1. At least one cabbage is edible.

2. One student at most pays for all drinks.

3. One and only one man is faithful.

4. Exactly one prisoner will be shot.

5. Two tourists at least will misunderstand.

6. At most two judges have exactly one ounce of intelligence.

7. Two runners will drop out.

8. If Peter loves Jane then at least two florists will be happy.

9. If exactly one computer crashes then exactly two technicians will be sacked.

10. If it is not the case that exactly one ice cream is soft then every ice cream will be eaten.

11. Either two people will leave in disgust or nobody will.

12. If exactly one person is reading and exactly two people are not, then there are exactly three people.

13. Exactly two husbands have at least three wives.

14. Between one and three people are not reading.

11.9   Will it ever end?

If a sentence is a logical necessity then, provided we do nothing silly, our tableau will end with contradictions on all branches (and vise versa). But since we may bring down a line more than once, if a sentence is not a logical necessity, our tableau for it may go on forever. Because the tableau will never hit a contradiction, we can keep bringing down lines again and again using new names each time. In many cases when we do a tableau for a sentence and do not hit a contradiction, we do not know whether this is because our tableau is not yet long enough or because the sentence is not in fact a logical necessity.

We *must* be allowed to bring down some lines indefinitely (we ignore the reason here). The tableaux system may be refined and improved. For example, if we are careful, then we will never need to bring down a restriced line more than once. However, this is not the case with unrestricted lines. This is not just a problem with the tableaux method. Actually, any deduction system at all, no matter how clever, will suffer from this problem in some form. This is a rather unpleasant fact, but unavoidable.

Appendix A

The complete tableau rules

Negation

T ~A	**F** ~A
F A	**T** A

Conjunction

T $A \cdot B$ F $A \cdot B$
T A
T B **F** A **F** B

Disjunction

T $A \vee B$ **F** $A \vee B$
                    F A
T A **T** B **F** B

Material Implication

T $A \supset B$ **F** $A \supset B$
                       T A
F A **T** B **F** B

Universal Quantification

T $(x)Fx$	**F** $(x)Fx$
T Fa	**F** Fa^*

Existential Quantification

T $(Ex)Fx$	**F** $(Ex)Fx$
T Fa^*	**F** Fa

Identity

Any sentence :   **T** $a = b$
T $a = a$ *a and b are now interchangeable.*

*The name used here must not have been used
anywhere above it in the same branch

Appendix B

Famous Truth Tables

~	A
F	T
T	F

·	A	B
T	T	T
F	T	F
F	F	T
F	F	F

∨	A	B
T	T	T
T	T	F
T	F	T
F	F	F

⊃	A	B
T	T	T
F	T	F
T	F	T
T	F	F

≡	A	B
T	T	T
F	T	F
F	F	T
T	F	F

|	A	B
F	T	T
T	T	F
T	F	T
T	F	F

Appendix C

A brief summary of Classical Logic

- An argument is valid when there is no way for the premises to be true while the conclusion is false. That is, when it is impossible (in a very strong sense of impossible) for the premises to be true and the conclusion to be false together (Def 1.1.2). See Sec 1.2 for examples.

- The truth value of a sentence is either true or false depending on whether the sentence in question is true or false.

- A truth functional sentence is a sentence which keeps its truth value the same when you exchange its embedded sentences (Def 2.1.1 is the definition of an embedded sentence) for any other sentence of the same truth value (Def 2.2.1).

- A truth function is what is left of a truth functional sentence after you have removed all its embedded sentences (Def 2.2.2).

- There are only five truth functions worth bothering about: conjunction, disjunction, negation, material implication, and material equivalence.

- We can express any sentence in formal logic by changing the truth functions for the ones described above and writing the embedded sentences as letters from the alphabet (usually capitals). See Sec 3.1.2 for examples.

-

Truth function	Symbol	Natural Language
Conjunction	$\cdot$	...and...
Disjunction	$\vee$	...or...
Negation	$\sim$	It is not the case that...
Material implication	$\supset$	If...then...(or, ...only if...)
Material equivalence	$\equiv$	...iff...(if and only if)

211

- The truth functions have truth tables that determine how they operate when the embedded sentences take various truth values:

Truth Function	Truth Table
·	Def 3.2.2
∨	Def 3.2.3
~	Def 3.2.1
⊃	Def 5.1.3
≡	Def 3.3.2

- A tautology is a sentence that is true no matter what truth values its embedded sentences take. Only sentences that are necessary in propositional logic are tautologies (Def 4.1.1).

- We can use truth tables to find tautologies (see Chapters 4 and 5).

- Watch out for counterfactuals, subjunctive implication sentences where the truth tables do not apply. See Sec 5.1.3 for explanation and examples.

- In predicate logic we introduce names and predicates (see Defs. 10.1.1 and 10.1.3).

- We also introduce quantifiers and variables which range over all existing objects. See Defs 10.4.1 and 10.4.2.

- There is no truth table system for predicate logic.

- In any predicate logic deduction system we may use each sentence more than once.

- Look at the chapters on tableaux for an advanced deduction system.

References

Philosophical Interest

1. Mark Sainsbury, *Logical Forms*, 2nd ed. (Blackwell, 2000).

   A book that covers all the philosophical issues ignored in this one.

2. R. Larson and G. Segal, *Knowledge of Meaning*, (MIT Press, 1996).

   A book that covers all the semantic issues ignored in this one.

3. G. Frege, *Begriffschift* (translated in *From Frege to Gödel*, Harvard, 1967).

   The Frege paper is of great historical interest but the anthology itself contains nothing but important works.

4. D. Gabbay and F. Guenthner, *Handbook of Philosophical Logic* (D. Reidel, 1983).

   Pretty much everything in here from the philosophical issues to the light and heavy logic. It comes in four volumes and is best read from a library.

Advanced Interest

1. M. Machover, *Set theory, Logic and Their Limitations* (CUP, 1996).

   A more advanced course on mathematical logic, in a slightly computational style. A very readable little book.

2. Mendelson, *Introduction to Mathematical Logic*, 3rd ed. (Wadsworth, 1987).

   An advanced course on mathematical logic in the older style.

3. J. Bell and M. Machover, *A Course in Mathematical Logic* (North-Holland, 1997).

   An advanced course in mathematical logic and set theory in every style imaginable (a BIG book).

4. Fitting and Mendelson, *First Order Modal Logic* (Kluwer, 1998).

   A book on modal logic containing Tableaux for modal logic.

5. G. Boolos and R. Jeffrey, *Computability and Logic* (CUP, 1991).

   An excellent book covering all the interesting and useful topics from a computational perspective. Very readable.

Alternative Interest (and some competition)

1. Copi and Cohen, *Introduction to Logic* (Prentice Hall, 1994).

   A classic that uses a deduction system different and older than Tableaux (though still a very common). Contains discussion of language related issues and fallacies.

2. W. Hodges, *Logic* (Penguin, 1977).

   Another classic using a slightly different Tableaux system. Contains discussion of issues in philosophical logic.

3. D. Gabbay, *Elementary Logics: a procedural perspective* (Prentice Hall, 1998)

   A book looking at many different systems of logic from the point of view of computation and application.

4. R. Lucas, *Mastering Prolog* (UCL, 1996).

   Prolog is a programming language that is geared to performing logical operations and deducing information from a database. It is based on predicate logic and may be thought of as a computer's understanding and application of validity. It is a very powerful and simple langauge.

Index

Invaluable People

The greatest of thanks go to the two people without whom this book would not have been possible:

Dov Gabbay
Tony Dale

I am also indebted the following people who offered me invaluable support and information:

Hans Jürgen 'M$_R$ LaTeX' Ohlbach
Moshe Machover
Donald Gillies
Yoshiko Umemori
Daniel Hill
Wassisname
John Woods
Valentine Shehtman
All the nerds at ESLII 97
All my colleagues at Kings (I know where you live)
Juliana 'Claudia' Cardinale
Jamie Gabbay
Medan Gabbay
'Raving' Rick Lewis
Larry Landau
Wilfried Meyer-Viol
Jane Spurr
Janice
Cleo

With extra special thanks to Lydia Rivlin for existing; the longer she maintains that property the better.

Also ultra extra special thanks go to me, without whose high opinion of my intelligence I should never have started this work.